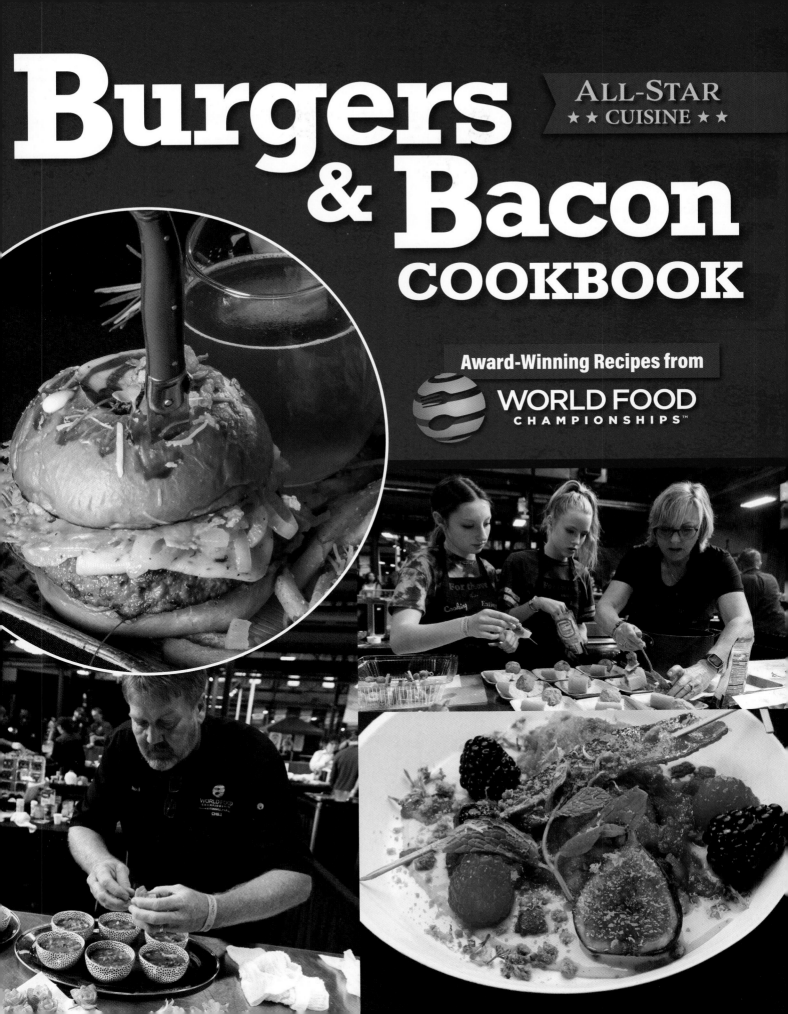

Burgers & Bacon

COOKBOOK

ALL-STAR
★ ★ CUISINE ★ ★

Award-Winning Recipes from

WORLD FOOD
CHAMPIONSHIPS™

Hardback: ISBN 978-1-4971-0446-4
Paperback: ISBN 978-1-4971-0455-6

Library of Congress Control Number: 2023950749

Photographs courtesy of www.Shutterstock.com:
Joshua Resnick (89)

To learn more about the other great books from Fox Chapel
Publishing, or to find a retailer near you, call toll-free
800-457-9112 or visit us at *www.FoxChapelPublishing.com*.

We are always looking for talented authors.
To submit an idea, please send a brief inquiry to
acquisitions@foxchapelpublishing.com.

Printed in China
First printing

ALL-STAR
★ ★ CUISINE ★ ★

Burgers & Bacon
COOKBOOK

OVER
250
WORLD'S BEST BURGERS, SAUCES, RELISHES & BUN RECIPES

Award-Winning Recipes from

WORLD FOOD
CHAMPIONSHIPS™

FOX CHAPEL
PUBLISHING

Acknowledgments

I want to thank everyone who has been involved and worked so hard
to make this cookbook a reality:

David Miller, Gretchen Bacon, David Fisk, Diana Kern, Aubrey Vonada,
Wendy Reynolds, Matthew Hartsock, Michele Sensenig, Erin Turner,
Lauren Younker, and everyone else at Fox Chapel Publishing.

Randall McCloud, Marcia Flatt, and Victoria Emrich from my team.

To the talented World Food Championship chefs
and finalists who contributed recipes.

To the hundreds of WFC staff, volunteers, spectators,
and fans. Our events wouldn't be possible without you.

—Mike McCloud, WFC Founder

Introduction

We are the World Food Championships, the leading food sport competition in the world since our debut in 2012. Culinary competitors who have qualified from all over the globe battle it out on our Kitchen Arena for a chance to win the ultimate food crown in 11 categories: Burgers, Bacon, BBQ, Steak, Seafood, Soups, Sandwiches, Desserts, Vegetarian, Rice/Noodles, and Live Fire. Glory and prize money aside, our week-long competition is also known as a springboard for chefs who are seeking TV fame and other major opportunities.

There's nothing else in the culinary world quite like the World Food Championships (WFC). The energy, the excitement, and the expertise are simply unmatched. And now, for the first time ever, you can bring the competition right into your very own kitchen with our very first official cookbook!

Within these pages, you'll find Top 10 Burger and Bacon recipes between 2018–2022, and even a few from this year's event. Special trophy symbols will identify first-place recipes from both categories. There are also symbols and sidebars that will help you discover alternative, more budget-friendly ingredients if what was used in the competitive recipe is too difficult to find. Also included are easy reference charts in the beginning of the book so you can easily pick and choose what you want to make if you're looking for a specific side, topping, sauce, jam, or other tasty component to try and serve however you wish.

While these recipes do require a bit of cooking experience, there's still something for everyone. Vegetarian or plant-based recipes are included, as well as desserts, seafood, comfort food, internationally inspired cuisine, and more.

Whether you've been to the World Food Championships as a competitor or a spectator, or you've always wanted to go, this cookbook is the perfect way to get a taste of the best food sporting event from home. We hope you build your cooking skills and learn something new, discover new, delicious favorites, and feel inspired to come up with your own recipes with the goal to qualify and compete! Until we see you in person, have fun and happy cooking.

CONTENTS

page 34 page 36 page 38 page 40
page 42 page 44 page 48 page 50

page 54   page 56   page 58   page 60
page 62   page 64   page 70   page 76

CONTENTS

page 108   page 114   page 118   page 120

page 124   page 128   page 130   page 132

page 134 · page 136 · page 138 · page 140

page 146 · page 154 · page 162 · page 166

EASY REFERENCE RECIPE CHART
Perfect Pairings and More to Cook
Your Own Culinary Masterpiece

Every winning recipe is made of more than just the bacon or the burger. There's something extra special within each perfect dish—whether it's a delicious relish, a savory sauce or spread, a crunchy topping, a homemade bun, or another addition—that makes each burger an award-winning recipe. This quick reference guide will help you find the special sauce, bun, or topping you want to recreate and use in your own original creations!

Sauces

Spreads

Special Toppings

Homemade Dressings, Seasonings, and Marinades

Sweet Treats, Sauces, and Creams

Jams

About the World Food Championships

Since its inception in 2012, the World Food Championships has hosted competitors from 49 of the 50 US states (all but Vermont!) and 40 countries, has launched the careers of more than 30 TV food stars, has awarded more than $3 million in prize money, and has connected more than 175 food brands with fans, bloggers, and media. The event has had notable airtime on several TV programs and networks, ranging from A&E and Food Network to Discovery, Destination America, and others. And while there's a lot to look forward to with the future of WFC, it's worth looking back at how it all began.

History of World Food Championships

It all started with barbecue.

Before there was a World Food Championships, there was a group of people with an idea. For years, WFC owner and founder, Mike McCloud, and his team were involved in competition barbecue with the Kansas City Barbecue Society, and they were eventually tasked with helping the organization grow. Nothing was off the table, so they began brainstorming ways to elevate barbecue competitions while also making them better for consumers. They soon realized that there was a lot more happening in the food competition scene beyond barbecue; events like Burger Battles, Sandwich Slams, and Chef Fights were popping up and gaining a lot of traction. And while there were already barbecue world champions out there, there weren't any world champions across those other food categories that the team was observing from afar. Then someone posed the question, "Why isn't there a championship of food event?" That was their "Eureka!" moment.

The concept was simple: take the best cooks in every category, put them all into the kitchen, and let them duke it out in the ultimate food fight. But after they landed on their idea, they then had to figure out how to make it happen and pull it off. And who? And where?

By 2010, the team was in game planning mode, establishing the rules to make the competition a level playing field across such different categories and thinking of a judging process. It was a challenge, navigating how they would compare the winner of desserts to the winner of barbecue—or one of the other seven categories they thought about—to then crown a World Food Champion. Their solution was the acronym EAT, which stood for execution (35%), appearance (15%), and taste (50%). They believed these three elements of a dish (and the breakdown of what each one was worth) was the best barometer in how to fairly score and judge dishes that could be so different.

Hello, Las Vegas

To show people they were serious about this event, the team knew they had to go big or go home, so the first-ever World Food Championship was held in 2012 at Caesars Palace in Las Vegas with Adam Richman as their celebrity host. By the time the 10 days were over (five of which were competition days), it was a roaring success and seven winners in seven categories went home as crowned champions. It was exciting, it was wild, and it filled a gap that was missing before: over 200 teams came out to compete, proving the people wanted this kind of a stage. The team knew they were onto something and got right back to work to discuss all of the new do's and don'ts they learned for next time.

Then and Now

What started as seven food categories has now become 12. And while Mike McCloud and his team are always striving for a bigger and better event than the last, they learned that doesn't always mean size. (Unless you're referring to the prize purse of course. That keeps growing!) In the first championship, there were over 200 teams competing that were made up of three to four people each. One year, they almost reached 500 teams, but learned that was too many. Since then, they've enforced a 20-team cap for each kitchen category (aside from Barbecue and Live Fire that have a 40-team maximum), landing on a sweet spot of just under 300 teams total. And because they've

tightened up parameters on the number of contestants, it has resulted in a harder bar of entry, making the competition (and victories) even more elite and prestigious!

It was also evolved into two major parts once participants get qualified to enter the World Food Championships (they must first win their way in through other events). November hosts the main event where teams try to win within their categories. Then, the winners from that event compete again in spring at a championship called The Final Table where they have a chance to win bonus money—a whopping $150,000 grand prize! There's so much in store and the future is bright for WFC as they continue to find ways to evolve, improve, and grow. From the volunteers and team who put it all together to the contestants and the spectators who come from all over, there's something special happening down in Houston, Texas. And at its core, it's all for the love of food.

CHECK IT OUT!

Scan the QR code below to watch a WFC Flashback video!

Behind the Scenes

A Cornucopia of People

When you enter the World Food Championships, you're sure to find a mix of people from all walks of life. Contestants range from ages 16 to 80, and in 2023, WFC Junior made its debut, which brought in even younger competitive chefs. Geographically, about 40 states are represented any given year, and on record, chefs from every state in the US has competed—except Vermont! Forty countries have also competed, and last year alone, five countries were represented in the Top 10 for Burgers. When it comes to training and experience, contestants fall within three main backgrounds: home cooks, competition teams, who do this as a serious hobby, and professional chefs—who can be classically trained, self-taught, an executive chef, or a James Beard nominee. But no matter anyone's experience level, one thing is certain: these chefs know how to cook, and they love it and live for it.

"It's those three legs of a stool that make up our competitive field. Ironically, it's about a third, a third, a third, so it's equally represented," says WFC owner and founder, Mike McCloud. And over the years, people from all three backgrounds have won, so it's anyone's game. A core philosophy of WFC is they don't care who you are, where you learned to cook, where you cook, or what you're a specialist at. If you can execute a great dish, you have as good a chance as anyone else to win. "For many reasons, it's called 'The American Idol of Food' because it's kind of a discovery process. I tend to think we see the next Guy Fieri's, the next Rachael Ray's, the next Paula Deen's of the world before anybody else does because we do have a fair and square way of getting into the game, getting onto the field, and getting seen and rewarded." People who have previously popped up out of nowhere onto the WFC scene have gone on to become a household name in the industry and achieve food fame. It's a land of opportunity where anything could happen, and WFC is setting the stage.

The Thrill of Victory

The excitement in the air is palpable. There's no doubt about how hard the contestants have worked, not only work during the competition, but also in the events that qualified them to compete. It's a long, winding road, and on announcing the winners, McCloud says, "I love the thrill of victory…It's always a phenomenal moment to see someone's dreams come true." What's more is seeing the same contestants compete every year, and then they eventually make it all the way through to the end as champion. McCloud has that awareness and history, watching and knowing their journeys, so when he gets to announce a contestant as a winner after they've competed for nine consecutive years, that adds an extra element of genuine pride and joy.

Aside from the climatic award ceremonies, what also makes the WFC a stand-out event are the lifelong friendships formed. The comradery is unmatched, and, as McCloud says, "It's like a bona fide high school reunion on steroids every year." During the welcome reception, hundreds of old friends gather and reunite who understand each other so well from competition, as well as the trials and tribulations of the industry. Add onto that just recently with COVID, supply chain shortages, staffing shortages, and a recession—they've been through it all. "People in this industry, I believe, are some of the most overworked and underappreciated people out there. When you get 1,200 of them together…watching them hug each other and catch up on each other's lives is a special moment."

Food is Love

Pause for a moment to think about football. You see coaches and players from the opposing team clap each other on the back, but that only happens after the game. During the game, every disadvantage one team has is an advantage for the other. But in food sport, that's not how it works. "It's a community event and phenomenon, and it's special to see how these people help each other and celebrate one another," says McCloud.

"I could tell you 100 stories if we had enough pages in a book of true food sport champions having helped someone right next to them who was missing an ingredient, and they were down to the last four or five minutes. They thought their game plan was destroyed, and then someone across the aisle, competing against them, hears what's going on and gives them a lemon or whatever it is they're missing because they have extra. They're trying to help their competitor finish because they know what it took to get here, and no one wants to see someone else disqualified. What everybody wants is to win on their own merit. Helping someone else out and up is not frowned upon in our sport. You don't see that much."

CHECK IT OUT!

Scan the QR code below to watch a WFC Flashback video!

Food always brings people together. When you make food for people, you're loving people, and feeding someone is taking care of them. So ultimately, it makes perfect sense there is such a spirit of companionship woven into what happens at the World Food Championships. And within the following pages, you'll notice that same spirit of comradery and community among the contributing chefs in their own words. In the next section, you'll read interviews both from Mike McCloud and a few of the featured chefs that encompass what it's like being a part of the food sport world.

INTERVIEWS

Team Croix Valley
Damon Holter

Interview with

Mike McCloud
FOUNDER OF WFC

Where does your love of food come from?

My childhood with my grandparents. All my memories of them involved big family gatherings with lots of yummy food, like biscuits, fried chicken, dumplings, and creamed corn. It's where I learned that food is love and love surrounds food.

How did you first get started in the food sport arena?

Through an opportunity to manage the marketing of a barbecue-sanctioning body. We dove deep into this and fell in love with food competitions. The barbecue arena was a mature vertical, but we simply thought that there could be a lot more with the right formatting: burgers, seafood, dessert, etc.

Can you explain how WFC was born?

As we looked around the landscape of food sport, we realized that there wasn't a true, global, universal type of competition that included numerous verticals with a big crowning moment. So, we began imagining how that might look. After about a year of planning, we developed a new scoring system, judging process, and a playoff system that would allow burger cooks to compete against sandwich specialists and grill masters of all types. And we knew that international teams would want to participate, thus, we branded our platform as the World Food Championships.

What's your favorite part of the event?
(Obvious answer: eating. What else?)

The cooks, hands down. We get to meet the most passionate and caring people in the world. When they bring their talents to our arena, it's like watching kids at a theme park. They're so excited, so happy, so thrilled to have a stage to excel upon, and that just drives their passion even more.

What's been a standout dish or favorite memory from WFC?

There are literally hundreds of moments that stand out! But I guess the one that I'll never forget is when Simon Majumdar told our 2013 champion that he had just tasted the best carrot cake of his life. That was an amazing moment that charted a new course for not only an amateur cook, but also for our event.

Since WFC has grown into a huge, televised event with big-name sponsors, what has that evolution been like to watch and manage over the years?

A roller coaster for sure, with lots of ups and downs and twists and turns. Early on, we were thrilled to have any company involved, as we tried to establish the largest prize purse in food sport. But now, it's more about strategic alignment on numerous levels. So that's been a great evolution that continues to motivate me and our team.

What excites you the most about the future of WFC?

Expansion. With 10 years under our belt, the question is no longer "is there a next year?" It's more like, where? What next? Products? International hosts? TV? Licensing? If you'll pardon the twist on a pun, it feels like we've just whetted our appetite for what's next.

Interview with

Anna Saunders (Davis)

Where does your passion for cooking come from?

Growing up on a farm and loving to use fresh vegetables, chicken, and beef. My parents encouraged me to explore new recipes, and at just eight and nine, I would write up long grocery lists for my mom to pick up ingredients for the dinner I was making that night. Soon, I began creating my own recipes, and this is where my passion for cooking really started taking flight.

What is your favorite dish to cook?

A savory, fresh, seasonal spring dish, picking foraged items to incorporate into it. And always savory. (I'm not a sweets chef at all!) Think seared halibut, creamy spring peas, wild chives, smoked crème fraîche, and white wine sauce.

How did you get started in food sport?

I began entering online recipe competitions in high school. Then I entered Chopped at Home and went to NYC to compete in-person for the finals. After winning this competition, I had the food sport bug and couldn't stop. That's what led me to find WFC.

How many years have you competed in WFC? Of those years, which stick out to you as your favorite/most memorable?

I've only competed in one so far, since COVID happened. But I feel like I've been in the WFC world for a long time because of all the wonderful connections and other cooking opportunities it has brought about. The excitement, the incredible support from chefs there, as well as family and friends, all the wonderful food smells—it's an experience you can never forget. I look forward to competing again in the future!

What advice would you give to someone new to cooking?

Always try something new. Don't aim for perfection every time, but rather let the mishaps be the foundation for learning. Be creative and never stop trying new flavors. If you can, travel! There are so many incredible cuisines around the world. Experience these firsthand and your inspiration will soar.

What advice would you give to someone who is interested in or new to competitive cooking?

1: Reach out to someone you know who has done competitive cooking. Seek advice and get some tips from them.

2: Always be creating new recipes and food. Anyone can practice to make perfect, or study to get labels, but no one can teach creativity. Your creativity is unique to you and is how you can stand out in a competition.

3: Think "inside the box" by reading up on competitions and think "outside the box" in how your dish could stand out in a crowd.

Interview with
Atsuko Ohgiya

Where does your passion for cooking come from?

My passion always comes from people's smiles. That is my one and the only reason to make me keep cooking with a passion and positive energy.

What is your favorite dish to cook?

No matter what I make (burgers or general dishes) my favorite step of cooking is to make sauces and dressings, which is a very fun moment to come up with a combination of several ingredients until confirming if the chemistry went well or not. It's always an adventure.

How did you get started in food sport?

Japan Burger Championship (JBC) 2022 was my first experience of food sport.

How many years have you competed in WFC? Of those years, which stick out to you as your favorite/most memorable?

It's been one year since I joined JBC. In both food sport and cooking in general, I realized how important it is to have fun with your teammates. I have been thinking how to make even more great dishes that people admire, and concluded that it can't be accomplished with only me or my skills, but I need supporters and teammates, and the most important part is they also need to have as much fun as I do.

What advice would you give to someone new to cooking?

To experience anything that you think you'll like! It might have nothing to do with cooking, but things you get inspired by can help you when you create dishes later on!

What advice would you give to someone who is interested in or new to competitive cooking?

"To be an entertainer." This is what I learned after I experienced my first food sport Japan Burger Championship and at the World Food Championships last year. It's a competition, so obviously you go there to fight, but at the same time, you can't forget that it's a show. You need to be a professional as a chef as well as an entertainer. It also helps you to act more freely in the kitchen booth where many of the audience members and cameras are watching you while you compete. Take it easy!

Interview with
Damon Holter

Where does your passion for cooking come from?

I've spent over 30 years surrounded by food; managing multiple restaurants, owning one with my family, and for the past 14 years, owning a food manufacturing business. I simply didn't fall into food as a passion, hobby or vocation, rather I grew up in a family who cooked made-from-scratch meals every day. It was learning to cook from my mother at a very young age that inspired me to share my interest in cooking and my interpretation of flavors with those around me.

What is your favorite dish to cook?

I can't say I have a favorite dish to cook. With the millions of edible items in this world, it's much too difficult to narrow down a favorite. What I do enjoy more than anything is creating new dishes, exploring different styles of cuisine, and experimenting with fusions of flavor, ingredients, and techniques. It's a pleasure to learn something new each time I cook and use that knowledge to develop new and exciting dishes along the way.

How did you get started in food sport?

When I first started Croix Valley, my focus for my business was in producing sauces and marinades for steak. I had a professional BBQ competitor reach out in search of a new BBQ sauce to use in the competition arena and I began developing new sauces tailored to the food sport palate. It wasn't but a few months into the project that I had to find out what competitive BBQ looked like and subsequently, I needed to give it a shot myself. One contest led to another, which led to even more, and a dozen years later, there's no stopping this competitive spirit!

How many years have you competed in WFC? Of those years, which stick out to you as your favorite/most memorable?

I've been competing at WFC since its second year, returning each year and cooking in variety of categories since I first discovered this venue. The most accomplished year for me was 2022 when I won the World

Sandwich Championship and was awarded the John Corey Spark Award. I set out with the goal of winning in mind and was fortunate enough to realize that milestone. While it was certainly the most successful competition year I've had, I have been a Top 10 competitor nearly every year I have competed, which always adds to the memories. I always tell everyone I meet that WFC is the pinnacle of food sport and the most cherished experience I look forward to each competition season, but the reasons why have more to do with the people I see and experiences I have than the actual competition itself. The food sport family is like no other, and the folks I have gotten to know in years of competition are what make it so memorable and give me the desire to return year after year.

What advice would you give to someone new to cooking?

My best advice for someone new to cooking is to not be intimidated by food. We certainly need food to survive, but we don't need tasty food to simply exist. Cooking food that tastes good is all about the experience and having a sense of accomplishment that you made something that you or those you're cooking for enjoy. I would tell anyone to embrace their ingredients, to not be afraid to experiment, to have the guts to toss the recipes aside and simply cook the way you want to cook, to entertain your senses with your dishes you create and to constantly learn new things.

What advice would you give to someone who is interested in or new to competitive cooking?

Competitive cooking is about having the confidence to be present and play a game. I have seen many first timers win their competitions by showing up, cooking what they like to cook and not being afraid to lose, and not feeling intimidated by the environment or the other competitors. Anyone can be a food sport competitor, but first and foremost, you simply have to believe in yourself.

Interview with

Joseph Martinez

Where does your passion for cooking come from?

My passion for cooking comes from my enjoyment of food. I was always in the kitchen with my parents and grandma as a child. As I grew older, I began to make meals for family dinner and helped out on the holidays. As time went on, I began to watch cooking shows and read books to continue learning.

What is your favorite dish to cook?

I absolutely love pasta. I've been making my own pasta from scratch for about eight years now. It's a calming and therapeutic practice that really makes me feel at peace. It's also a great comfort food.

How did you get started in food sport?

I began competing when I was in my early 20s. It began by entering online recipe contests. After three consecutive wins, I began competing in San Antonio at local food festivals and competitions. After winning a Burger Championship consecutively against 10 other local chefs, I was presented the ticket to compete at the World Food Championships.

How many years have you competed in WFC? Of those years, which stick out to you as your favorite/most memorable?

I've only competed once in 2022, but I'm absolutely hooked on it. It was such an incredible experience and meeting so many individuals and chefs from around the world was impactful. The fact that Team Tributary made it to the finals on our very first year was also really special. We definitely had an amazing time!

What advice would you give to someone new to cooking?

The best advice I could give to anyone is don't be afraid to make mistakes. No one perfects a recipe or technique the first time. It's important to remember that everything gets better with practice, so if something doesn't turn out the way you wanted it to or the way the recipe shows, try again. Repetition is the mother of all skill. It's important to remember that when cooking.

What advice would you give to someone who is interested in or new to competitive cooking?

When it comes to competitive cooking, it's important to remember to have fun with it. It's really easy to get lost in the competitive side of things, but most people, including myself, perform much better when I'm having fun and enjoying what I'm doing as opposed to stressing over winning.

Interview with
Stephen Coe

Where does your passion for cooking come from?

My passion for cooking comes from growing up in the hospitality industry. From the age of eight, I was filling donuts. I was surrounded by fearless chef mentors that pushed us to be the best and never stop hustling! And then I got the taste of competitions when I was 12 years old and never turned back. I live to compete.

What is your favorite dish to cook?

My favorite dish to cook is my deconstructed rabbit or my free form lobster ravioli that took down Bobby Flay in a Chopped tournament.

How did you get started in food sport?

I started competing at the age of 12 with VICA, ACF, DECA, and Skills USA.

How many years have you competed in WFC? Of those years, which stick out to you as your favorite/most memorable?

I'm an 8-year veteran to WFC, and 2015 was the best, as we took World Bacon Category.

What advice would you give to someone new to cooking or competitive cooking?

I tell people to ask all the questions, take notes, keep your head down and your eyes open, hustle hard, and jump into the fire. Play hard, train hard!

Interview with
Susanne Duplantis

Where does your passion for cooking come from?

I grew up on a step stool in my MeMaw's (grandmother's) kitchen, I was her sous chef before I ever knew that term. She loved to cook and her passion for cooking and for valuing food was instilled in me at a young age. The kitchen is my happy place. I cook from the heart and cooking is an act of love for me.

What is your favorite dish to cook?

My favorite dish is my MeMaw's Maque Choux, or smothered corn. Just about any meat, seafood, or vegetables can be added, making it so versatile, it goes with just about anything, and it uses up all parts of fresh corn for no food waste, which is my mission. My MeMaw added a bit of bacon fat to hers. I used to love to eat the cold Maque Choux leftovers on a hot dog as a kid.

How did you get started in food sport?

I was an athlete all throughout school and into college. I love a good competition. So, while I was in the restaurant industry for 22 years, I always enjoyed competitive cooking events whether for charity or titles. A good competition brings out the best in me. So when I was told about WFC, I just knew I had to get involved. I love the adrenaline rush the timed food sport competition with the top cooks and chefs in the world gives me. It is full speed ahead just like a college basketball game!

How many years have you competed in WFC? Of those years, which stick out to you as your favorite/most memorable?

I competed in the first WFC Food Fight Write event (which was steak) and then went on to compete in three World Food Championships, two burgers and one chili. They all hold a special place in my heart, but I would have to say it was the 2018 WFC when I placed in the top ten for burger and won the Blended Burger Competition. There is

nothing like hearing your name called twice and all of my family was in attendance to celebrate with me. It also was the first time I met my sous chefs and we cooked together like a group that has been cooking together for years. We just clicked and had the best time, and we still do.

What advice would you give to someone new to cooking?

Step out of your comfort zone. Try new things. Even a mess can turn into a success. Get creative and, most importantly, have fun.

What advice would you give to someone who is interested in or new to competitive cooking?

Practice as much as possible and practice with a clock running. Good prepping and organization of ingredients and equipment is key. Be precise in writing steps needed to be completed by what time to stay ahead of the clock game and give you insight to your time management. Taste as you go and make adjustments as needed. Breathe and enjoy the experience.

Competition Rules

Feeling inspired? Below is a preview of the competition rules you can expect when you become a contestant at the World Food Championships!

1. A competitor is defined as a head cook. Head cooks must be at least 18 years of age at the time of the competition OR they must have written consent from a parent or legal guardian who is present with them in Kitchen Arena at all times during the competition.

2. Competitors (head cooks) may have assistants during the competition period.

3. The World Food Championships will consist of ten (10) to twelve (12) official categories, for which there will be at least two (2) Rounds of competition:

4. An Opening Round in which a maximum of 20 contestants per category will have one hour and thirty minutes (1.5 hours) to create their Signature Dish. Certain ingredients and/or products may be required and will be communicated to contestants prior to the Recipe deadline.

5. A Final Round in which seven (7) contestants in each category will advance and will have one hour and thirty minutes (1.5 hours) to create ONE (1) dish. Certain ingredients and/or products may be required and will be communicated to contestants prior to the Recipe deadline. Unlike the Opening Round judging process, the Final Rounds will follow a LIVE PANEL judging process.

6. To ensure competitor fairness, as well as the judges' safety and allergy concerns, all cooks in the Opening Rounds will be required to submit a Dish Description for their Signature Dish.

7. All competitor entries must be original creations and not the property rights of any third party.

8. Competitors may, but are not required, to recreate any entry that allowed them to win qualification into the World Food Championships.

9. The use of sponsored products is a requirement if stated by WFC's competition chart and process.

10. Golden Tickets for qualifying and no-cost entries for champions, may NOT be transferred to another person.

11. Competitors can enter and win multiple qualifiers to the WFC.

12. WFC reserves the right to enter into exclusive agreements with events that allow them to become the only WFC qualifying event in a state, province and/or country.

13. Registration Period Payment MUST be made at the time of registration. Registration fees are non-refundable.

14. Any competitor who has claimed a spot at the World Food Championships through a completed registration is expected to be present and to compete at the event.

15. On-site registration for both the Opening and the Final Round is required for all competitors. The head cook must be present, no exceptions.

16. Competitor entries and recipes for the E.A.T™ blind-judging portion in the Opening Round cannot be marked or designated in any way that uniquely identifies to the judges who has submitted the entry.

17. All competition entries must be prepared onsite during the tournament period. This rule also applies to decor and garnish intended to decorate your turn-in tray. No pre-chopping of ingredients, mise en place, previously cooked or prepared entries will be accepted or allowed. 16. Any and all fresh meat, fish or seafood brought to the tournament must be packaged in a USDA approved facility with a proper USDA stamp. Live shellfish such as oysters, lobster, and clams, are allowed to be used and brought into Kitchen Arena unwrapped or unpackaged, as we consider it to be in its own "nature's packaging." These items will be required to be stored under safe and sanitary conditions, and a receipt for proof of purchase will be required.

18. Entries may include any combination of ingredients, sauces, toppings, or decor/garnishes. 18. For sanitary purposes and the health/safety of our judges, all entries and samples must be plated.

19. Proper food safety guidelines should always be followed.

20. All food must be placed on or in a solid dish that can be picked up with one hand.

21. No part of an entry, including but not limited to plate ware, food, garnish/decor, will be allowed to extend beyond 3 inches off the edges of the turn-in platter.

22. WFC will provide each competitor in Kitchen Arena with a basic equipment/cooking package. Competitors are allowed to bring the following small appliances, as long as the equipment fits inside their cooking station: blender, hand immersion blender, hand mixer, food processor, waffle iron, ice cream maker, stand mixer and small spice/coffee grinder. If a piece of electrical equipment is NOT on the list, you may NOT use it during your competition. No personal grills or smokers will be allowed in Kitchen Arena.

23. All Opening Round competitors will be required to create:
    a. One (1) presentation plate and five (5) sampling portions of their Signature dish for E.A.T.™ Judging
    b. Portions for a People's Choice judging program

24. Unless otherwise modified in the Competitor Packets, all Final Round competitors of a category will be required to create one (1) presentation dish and ten (10) sampling portions. Five (5) of the entries during the Final Round will be used to taste and score by the panel of five (5) judges, while the additional five (5) samples will go into the Judge's Lounge for back up, extra tasting, and possible photography by WFC officials.

25. As contemplated in Rule 24, during the Final Round, all competitors will be given two (2) silver platters for the turn-in process. Both platters must be turned in with the competitor's entry.

26. Once numbered trays have been issued, each head cook is responsible for his/her tray. Any marked or altered tray must be replaced prior to turn-in, or it will be disqualified.

27. CAUTION: a competitor is NOT finished with turn-in until BOTH trays are set down.

28. During the Opening Round, competitors may not discuss recipes, ingredients, or convey a description of their dish to any judge participating in the E.A.T™ Blind Judging Portion at any point before their competition times. Likewise, judges participating in the E.A.T™ Blind Judging Portion may not observe competitors as they cook during the rounds they are judging, as this is a blind competition. Any judge doing so will be removed from their duties as a judge. This rule does not apply to Master Judges in the Opening Round.

29. Each year's categorical Final Round Finishers earn automatic qualification for the next year's event and are eligible to register during the Early Bird Registration period. After that, Final Round Finishers may still choose which category they wish to compete in, but spots are only available on a first-come, first-served basis. This qualification does not include the entry fee.

30. Each year's Category Champions earn automatic qualification into the tournament for the next five (5) years. As a Champion, this rule also provides a no-cost entry for that Champion into next year's tournament. As with Final Round Finishers, Category Champions are eligible to register during the Early Bird Registration period. After that, Category Champions may still choose which category they wish to compete in, but spots are only available on a first-come, first-served basis. To continue earning a no-cost entry throughout the five-year qualified period, the person would have to win the category he/she competes in each previous year.

31. Any World Food Champion (1st place finisher at the Final Table) earns a lifetime exemption into the tournament. For the first five (5) successive years, the World Food Champion will also earn a no-cost entry into the tournament. Beginning year six (6), and each successive year thereafter, entry fees will not be waived. World Food Champions can select any category they want during their exemption period and are eligible to register during the Early Bird Registration period.

32. Throughout the course of the competition, immediate family members (spouses, brothers, sisters, fathers, sons, mothers, daughters, grandparents and grandchildren) may compete individually in the same category or opposing categories through Opening Round and Final Round and may even win separate categories. However, multiple members of the same family may not be represented at the Final Table unless they are on ONE (1) team. Therefore, if members of the same family should win in two (2) different categories, the member who was announced first shall advance to the Final Table. The family member who wins the second category shall be awarded the prize purse for his/her first-place finish in their category. However, the second highest scorer in that category will advance to the Final Table. Additionally, that second family member will then be allowed to compete with the first family member on the same team at the Final Table. The purpose of this rule is to prevent any possible collusion or appearance of collusion at the Final Table by family members representing multiple teams.

33. Team/contestant branded apparel and signage is allowed in your team's work stations and in your competitor area, as long as it is not perceived as disruptive, offensive, concerning, or conflicting by WFC officials and its sponsors. In such cases, WFC reserves the right to remove such signage or branding.

34. Corporate sponsorship of any contestant constitutes a Brand Team. Brand Teams must be approved by WFC Officials prior to the event.

35. Competitors must be courteous and respectful at all times. Competitors should never obstruct pathways within Kitchen Arena or interfere with another competitor's turn-in. Doing so could result in a disqualification for careless behavior.

36. Violation of any of the foregoing rules can and may result in elimination from the tournament. There will be no refund of entry fees for any rules infraction.

37. Head cooks MUST attend the mandatory cook's meeting. Other team members may not serve as proxy. If needed, an interpreter may be present with the head cook at the cook's meeting if English is not their first language. Absence of the head cook from the cook's meeting will result in a one (1) point deduction from the team's overall score.

38. WFC has implemented a Points Deduction process to address any possible infractions to the rules herein. Cheferees will bring potential infractions to the attention of the Head Cheferee. Only the Head Cheferee or a WFC Official may assign penalties. The severity of the infraction will determine the amount of points deducted, or if a team disqualification is necessary.

39. WFC exercises a zero-tolerance policy for threatening behavior, hate speech or drug/alcohol use during the competition. If exhibited, competitors are subject to immediate disqualification as well as permanent expulsion from attending or competing at any future World Food Championship event.

40. All head cooks and assistants participating in WFC competitions or activities realize and accept personal responsibility for the potential of personal harm involved with cooking and competing in a high stress environment. As such, all head cooks are required to sign indemnification waivers on their own behalf and on behalf of their assistants upon registering to compete at WFC. WFC reserves the right to require ALL assistants to sign waivers upon arrival at the competition.

41. All WFC decisions are final.

42. If the head cook has any specific questions or needs clarification regarding these rules, please email your questions to *champchat@worldfoodchampionships.com*.

43. All rules herein are subject to change. When significant changes occur, WFC will make competitors aware through email and/or web site and social updates. As a result, it is the responsibility of the competitor to regularly check the WFC website for any changes to the Official Competition Rules and Competitor Packets.

the BURGERS

Head Cook:
Dave Elliott

Team Name:
Porky McBeef and the Cluckers
Olathe, KS

Business Name:
PMB Barbecue Co.

Facebook:
DaveElliottBBQ

Instagram:
@FoodChampDave
www.PMBBarbecueCo.com

This is a recipe that I initially came up with a few years ago. It has evolved quite a bit since then, with the only original element being the bourbon bacon jam. The most significant evolution of this dish probably occurred between the opening round and the final round at the 2022 World Food Championships. This burger begins with fresh ground ribeye, chuck, and a short-rib patty infused with hickory smoked bacon on a fresh-baked brioche bun with lemon herb aioli and arugula. Topped with bourbon bacon jam, Gruyère cheese, and a runny egg. Served with fresh-made pickles.

Cook Time: 1 Hour | Makes 4-6 servings

Ingredients

FRESH-MADE PICKLES:

3 small cucumbers

½ cup vinegar

1 tablespoon dill

Dash of all-purpose seasoning (I used 2 Gringos Chupacabra Special Blend)

BOURBON BACON JAM:

1½ pounds bacon

2 cups shallots, finely chopped

1 cup sweet onion, finely chopped

4 cloves garlic, finely chopped

1 teaspoon chili powder

½ teaspoon paprika

½ cup bourbon

½ cup maple syrup

¼ cup balsamic vinegar

½ cup light brown sugar

LEMON HERB AIOLI:

¾ cup mayonnaise (I used Duke's Mayonnaise)

1 teaspoon lemon juice

½ teaspoon garlic, cooked

½ teaspoon rosemary

½ teaspoon parsley

RUNNY EGG:

1 egg, per burger

Dash of poultry seasoning (I used 2 Gringo's Chupacabra Cluckalicious)

Dash of paprika

BURGERS:

8-ounce ribeye, chuck, and short-rib patty, per burger

Brisket rub, to taste (I used 2 Gringos Chupacabra Brisket Magic)

⅛ cup arugula, per burger

1 slice Gruyère cheese, per burger

BUNS:

Brioche buns

1 stick butter

All-purpose seasoning (I used 2 Gringos Chupacabra Chop Haus Blend)

3 sprigs rosemary

2 cloves garlic, diced

Directions

FRESH-MADE PICKLES:

1. Slice cucumbers into ⅛-inch slices and place into a bowl.
2. Add garlic, dill, and a dash of all-purpose seasoning.
3. Pour vinegar over cucumbers. Stir.
4. Refrigerate for 30 minutes.

BOURBON BACON JAM:

1. Cook the bacon in two frying pans to allow for room for it to crisp up properly. Cook over medium heat until it browns perfectly. You want the bacon a little crisper with as little visible fat as possible. Transfer to paper towels to drain excess fat.
2. Leave about 1 to 2 tablespoons of bacon fat in one of the pans.

3. Add finely chopped shallots and onion to the pan and cook over medium heat until they start to caramelize.
4. Add the garlic and cook for about one more minute.
5. Add the chili powder and paprika, stir to combine.
6. Increase heat to high and add the bourbon (carefully) and maple syrup. Bring to a boil, stir, and scrape the pan so all the little bacon bits come loose. Continue boiling for about 2 to 3 minutes.
7. Add vinegar and brown sugar and continue to boil for about 3 minutes.
8. Using a sharp knife, cut the bacon into small pieces.

9. Toss the bacon into the pan, reduce heat to low, and simmer for about 10 minutes. The mixture will thicken and look jam-like in the process.
10. Turn off the stove top. Drain any excess fat off the bacon jam by pouring it through cheesecloth to drain it.

LEMON HERB AIOLI:

1. Place mayonnaise into bowl.
2. Add 1 teaspoon of lemon juice and mix.
3. Finely chop ½ teaspoon of rosemary, ½ teaspoon of parsley, and ½ teaspoon of cooked garlic. Stir into mixture.

Don't be afraid to try something new. Whether it is cooking a new dish, or entering a competition for the first time, have fun with it! Practice can be delicious!"

—Dave Elliott

DIRECTIONS CONTINUED

RUNNY EGG:

1. Cook egg so the yolk is runny.

2. Lightly season and add a dash of paprika for color.

BURGERS:

1. Form 8-ounce patties using the beef mixture.

2. Season with brisket rub to taste.

3. Cook patties on a medium-high grill to sear.

4. Remove and finish in oven to 129°F.

5. Place one slice of Gruyère on each patty.

BUNS:

1. Preheat oven to 350°F.

2. Slice buns in half and toast in oven.

3. Melt a stick of butter in pan.

4. Add rosemary, all-purpose seasoning, and 2 cloves of diced garlic.

5. Spread butter onto cut side of bun crown.

ASSEMBLY:

1. Spread 2 teaspoons of aioli onto cut side of bottom bun.

2. Layer ⅛ cup arugula on top of aioli.

3. Place patty with Gruyère on top of arugula.

4. Spread 2 tablespoons of bourbon bacon jam on top of Gruyère.

5. Put the runny egg on top of bourbon bacon jam.

6. Place crown of bun on top of egg.

7. Serve with fresh-made pickles.

Bacon Avocado Cheeseburger

Head Cook:
Suzanne Burton

Team Name:
Hot, Thick & Juicy
Madison, AL

A juicy burger dressed with chunky avocado, bacon, provolone cheese, green leaf lettuce, and sriracha mayo on a toasted brioche bun.

Cook Time: 30 Minutes | Makes 12 servings

Ingredients

EASY AVOCADO SPREAD:

2 8-ounce containers of chunky avocado spread

1 14.5-ounce can of petite diced tomatoes (I used Red Gold Petite Diced Tomatoes with Green Chilies)

1 jalapeño, seeded and diced

1 teaspoon all-purpose seasoning (I used Boars Night Out White Lightning Grill Seasoning)

1 lime, juiced

SRIRACHA MAYO:

1 cup mayonnaise

3 tablespoons sriracha sauce (or to your desired level of heat)

BURGERS:

Nonstick vegetable oil spray, for the grill

12 5.33-ounce burger patties (I used Bo Jackson's Burger Patties)

12 ounces Wagyu ground beef ($^{80}/_{20}$)

1 tablespoon BBQ seasoning (I used Rebel Rub)

1 tablespoon all-purpose seasoning (I used Boars Night Out White Lightning, plus extra for seasoning the outside of the patty)

1 tablespoon steak seasoning (I used Weber Steak 'n Chop)

1 tablespoon steak seasoning (I used Killer Hogs Steak Rub, plus extra for seasoning the outside of the patty)

24 strips bacon, cooked

12 slices provolone cheese

12 pieces green leaf lettuce

12 slices tomato

12 brioche buns, toasted

1 stick butter (I used Challenge Salted Butter)

1 tablespoon garlic powder

12 multi-colored cherry tomatoes, for topping

12 baby dill pickles, for topping

TIP:

- You can substitute Wagyu ground beef with ground top ribeye steak or any other ground heavily marbled meat with a high fat content.

Directions

EASY AVOCADO SPREAD:

1. Combine the chunky avocado, diced tomatoes, diced jalapeño, seasoning, and lime juice in a bowl.
2. Set aside.

SRIRACHA MAYO:

1. Combine the mayo and sriracha sauce in a small bowl.
2. Set aside.

BURGERS:

1. **Make the bacon:**
2. Render the bacon in a pan over medium heat until crispy; set aside on paper towels.
3. **Make the buns:**
4. Melt the stick of butter in a microwave-safe bowl. With a brush, baste the inside of the bun with butter and sprinkle each half lightly with garlic powder. Toast the inside of the buns in a skillet over medium heat.
5. **Make the burgers:**
6. Preheat a gas grill to high heat and coat the grates with vegetable oil spray.
7. Combine the burger patties, Wagyu ground beef, and seasonings in a large bowl.
8. Mix with your hands until just combined.
9. Form 12 burger patties.
10. Lightly sprinkle with all-purpose seasoning on both sides of the patty. Cook until the burger reaches an internal temperature of 155°F.
11. Just before you remove it from the grill, put a piece of provolone cheese on top.
12. Then remove from heat and let rest for 10 minutes.

ASSEMBLY:

1. Dress both sides of each bun with sriracha mayo.
2. Place a piece of green leaf lettuce on the bottom bun.
3. Next, place a burger patty with provolone cheese.
4. Put 1 slice of tomato and top with 1 tablespoon of avocado spread.
5. Lay 2 strips of bacon crossed.
6. Place the top bun on each burger.

"Cooking is a philosophy; it's not a recipe."
—Marco Pierre White

Bang Bang Double Cheeser

Head Cook:
George Przybylski

Team Name:
Bang Bang BBQ
Wilmington, DE

Facebook: Bang Bang BBQ
Competition Cooking Team

Instagram:
@BangBangBBQ

The inspiration for this burger came from many places, from a side dish at a local restaurant, to my son's love of smoked Gouda, to an incredible random find and obsession with black garlic. We wanted a burger that hit all areas of the tongue at the precise times, from the sweet and spicy bacon jam to the tangy peppery lemon-dressed arugula to the earthy sweet unami of the black garlic aioli. We loaded the double burger patties with an incredible smoked Gouda cheese sauce to tie it all together.

Cook Time: 45 Minutes | Makes 6 servings

Ingredients

BLACK GARLIC AIOLI:

1 cup mayonnaise

1 bulb black garlic

1 teaspoon black lava sea salt

SPICY BACON JAM:

1 pound bacon (I used Wright Brand Bacon)

2 tablespoons bacon grease

1 jalapeño, diced

3 medium sweet onions, diced

4 small shallots, diced

2 tablespoons smoked paprika

½ cup water

⅓ cup maple syrup

½ cup apple cider vinegar

½ cup brown sugar

SMOKED GOUDA CHEESE SAUCE:

8 ounces smoked Gouda cheese

¼ stick butter

⅛ cup flour

1 cup heavy cream

1 cup whole milk

ARUGULA DRESSING:

1 bag baby arugula

Juice of 1 medium lemon

⅛ cup olive oil

1 tablespoon black lava sea salt

BURGERS:

3 pounds burger meat blend (Equal amounts of ground chuck, brisket, and short rib. 80/20 fat ratio)

BBQ seasoning, to taste (I used BBQ Buddha Steak Zen Seasoning)

Black pepper, to taste

6 ciabatta rolls

TIP:

- You can substitute black lava sea salt with Himalayan pink salt or regular sea salt.

Black Garlic Substitute Recipe

1. Roast 1 bulb of garlic.

2. Cut in half and rub with olive oil.

3. Wrap tightly in foil and bake at 350°F for 20–30 minutes.

4. Add a few drops of balsamic vinegar to the cloves when cooled.

Directions

BLACK GARLIC AIOLI:

1. Shell 1 head of black garlic onto plate and mash into a paste.

2. Put mayonnaise into bowl with lemon juice, salt, and black garlic. Stir to incorporate. Place in fridge until needed.

ARUGULA DRESSING:

1. Dress arugula with juice of lemon, olive oil, and black lava sea salt.

2. Place in fridge until needed.

SPICY BACON JAM:

1. Place jalapeño on hot grill and roast until charred.

2. Cook bacon in a large, heavy bottomed pot until brown and mostly crisp.

3. Remove bacon and place on a paper towel-lined plate and set aside.

4. Remove all but 2 tablespoons of bacon grease and sauté onion and shallots over low to medium heat, stirring often.

5. Cook onions until soft and translucent, about 8 minutes.

6. Add smoked paprika and stir until fully incorporated.

7. Add water and scrape any brown bits at the bottom of the pan.

8. Add maple syrup, brown sugar, cooked bacon, diced jalapeño, and vinegar. Bring to a boil and let cook until a bit of a glaze forms, about 10–15 minutes.

9. Add mixture to the bowl of a food processor and pulse several times until a chunky jam consistency is obtained.

SMOKED GOUDA CHEESE SAUCE:

1. Grate smoked Gouda.

2. Heat butter in pan. Once melted, add flour and stir to create roux.

3. Add heavy cream and milk.

4. Heat to almost boil and add grated smoked Gouda cheese. Keep adding until a thick sauce is formed.

5. Remove from heat.

BURGERS:

1. Form beef into 6 patties and season with BBQ seasoning.

2. Grill until medium-well doneness, approximately 4–5 minutes per side on medium-high heat.

3. Cut rolls in half and toast on grill.

ASSEMBLY:

1. Bottom roll
2. Bacon jam
3. Beef patty
4. Cheese sauce
5. Beef patty
6. Cheese sauce
7. Arugula
8. Black garlic aioli on top bun
9. Top sandwich
10. Enjoy!

"Cooking is all about people. Food is maybe the only universal thing that has the power to bring people together. No matter the culture, everywhere around the world, people eat together."

—Guy Fieri

Head Cook:
Derrick Madaris

Team Name:
Croix Valley
Roberts, WI

Facebook:
Derrick Madaris

A molten béchamel burger bun, which is a hollowed-out bun filled with a luxurious béchamel sauce. This is designed to infuse every bite with explosive flavor when it's cut in half! An elegant yet simple Impossible Meat burger that includes a smokey jackfruit jam, a smooth garlic crème fraiche, beer cheese, beer onions, micro greens, my signature burger sauce, herb cheese, crispy onions, garlic and herb sauce, and a beautiful béchamel.

Cook Time: 1 Hour | Makes 4–6 servings

Ingredients

BACON JACKFRUIT JAM:

½ cup jackfruit, diced

1 red onion, thinly sliced

1 tablespoon liquid smoke

1 teaspoon chipotle chili powder

2 tablespoons brown sugar

3 tablespoons apple cider vinegar

2 tablespoons onion chutney

GARLIC CRÈME FRAICHE:

4 ounces sour cream

1 tablespoon garlic seasoning (I used Croix Valley Garlic Booster)

1 teaspoon minced garlic

SIGNATURE BURGER SAUCE:

1 cup mayonnaise

2 tablespoons ketchup

2 small dill pickles, chopped

1 tablespoon pickle juice

Squeeze of lemon juice

¼ onion, diced

1 tablespoon butter

Salt and pepper, to taste

BÉCHAMEL SAUCE:

¼ cup + 2 tablespoons butter

¼ cup + 2 tablespoons flour

2¼ cups heavy cream

1 tablespoon garlic seasoning (I used Croix Valley Garlic Booster)

⅔ cup beer (I used Boulevard beer)

1 cup sharp cheddar cheese, shredded

2 teaspoons BBQ sauce (I used Croix Valley Barbeque and Brat Sauce)

Salt and pepper, to taste

BEER ONIONS:

1 onion, sliced

1 tablespoon butter

¼ cup beer (I used Boulevard beer)

PARMESAN CRISPS:

Parmesan cheese, freshly grated

PLANT-BASED BURGERS:

1½ pounds plant-based meat (I used Impossible Meat)

1 tablespoon canola oil

Garlic seasoning, to taste (I used Croix Valley Garlic Booster)

Salt and pepper, to taste

1 sprig thyme

½ sprig rosemary

3 cloves garlic, minced

2 tablespoons butter

4–6 slices garden herb Gouda cheese

Microgreens

TIP:

- You can substitute jackfruit with seitan, tempeh, tofu, or portobella mushrooms.

Directions

BACON JAM:

1. Sauté diced jackfruit over low heat, along with red onion and add to the pot.
2. After onions get translucent, add liquid smoke, chipotle chili powder, brown sugar, apple cider vinegar, and onion chutney. Simmer over low heat until jam-like.

GARLIC CRÈME FRAICHE:

1. Mix sour cream with garlic seasoning and minced garlic.

SIGNATURE BURGER SAUCE:

1. Mix mayonnaise, ketchup, chopped dill pickles, pickle juice, and a squeeze of lemon juice.

2. Add chopped onion to pan and sauté with butter.
3. Caramelize and add to sauce, mix, season with salt and pepper.

BÉCHAMEL SAUCE:

1. Melt 2 tablespoons butter in a heavy-bottomed saucepan.
2. Stir in 2 tablespoons flour and cook, stirring constantly, until the paste cooks and bubbles a bit, but don't let it brown—about 2 minutes.
3. Add 1¼ cups hot heavy cream, continuing to stir as the sauce thickens. Bring it to a boil.
4. Add salt and pepper to taste, lower the heat, and cook, stirring for 2 to 3 minutes more.

5. Remove from the heat. To cool this sauce for later use, cover it with wax paper or pour a film of heavy cream over it to prevent a skin from forming.
6. Melt ¼ cup butter and 1 tablespoon garlic seasoning over medium heat in a saucepan. Cook 1 minute.
7. Stir in ⅔ cup beer and 1 cup heavy cream a bit at a time, whisking until smooth after each addition. Continue cooking over medium heat until thick and bubbly.
8. Reduce heat to low, add cheese, and stir just until melted and smooth.

BEER ONIONS:

1. Thinly slice onion and add to a pot over medium heat with butter.

> "The secret of good cooking is, first, having a love of it."
> —James Beard

DIRECTIONS CONTINUED

2. Cook until translucent and add beer. Cook for roughly 5 minutes.

PARMESAN CRISPS:

1. Heat oven to 350°F and place parchment paper on a baking sheet.

2. Spread freshly grated parmesan cheese into circles the size of the bun.

3. Bake for 10 minutes or until it looks golden on the bottom.

PLANT-BASED BURGER:

1. Heat cast iron pan on high heat and add canola oil.

2. Form meat into patties, place in cast iron, and season with garlic booster.

3. Cook one side for roughly 3 minutes, flip, and season with salt and pepper. Cook for 1 minute.

4. Kill the heat but leave on stove top. Add on sliced garden herb Gouda, thyme, rosemary, minced garlic, and butter to center of pan. Let it start to crackle, then tilt pan down and baste onto top of burger with spoon until cheese is melted.

5. With the top bun, cut a hole in the center (be careful not to pierce the other side of the bun) then toast both buns in the garlic herb butter on cast iron pan while it's still hot.

ASSEMBLY:

1. Bottom bun
2. Burger sauce
3. Microgreens
4. Burger with herb cheese
5. Sautéed onions
6. Bacon jam
7. Beer cheese
8. Crispy onions
9. Top bun with crème fraiche on bottom
10. Place top bun; spoon in béchamel in hole on top
11. Drizzle garlic and herb butter
12. Serve with knife in the middle and cut before eating

Bo's Spicy Avocado Burger

Head Cook:
Karen Elliott

Team Name:
Pirates of the Grillibbean
Bartlett, TN

Facebook:
Pirates of the Grillibbean

Instagram:
@PiratesOfTheGrillibbean

This recipe is a made with Bo Jackson's Grand Slam burger meat blended with pork chorizo and ground beef, topped with Havarti jalapeño cheese, roasted jalapeño slices, honey-coated bacon, avocado crispy chips, and crumbles of Cotija cheese sitting on lettuce and chow chow relish, all supported by a buttered toasted brioche bun, spread with avocado remoulade sauce.

Cook Time: 30 Minutes | Makes 4–6 servings

Ingredients

AVOCADO REMOULADE SAUCE:

1¾ cups mayonnaise

¾ cup chunky avocado spread

2 tablespoons horseradish mustard

2 teaspoons hot sauce

1 tablespoon garlic, minced

2 teaspoons jarred jalapeño juice

2 teaspoons taco seasoning

AVOCADO CRISPY CHIPS:

½ cup chunky avocado spread

¾ cup grated parmesan cheese

¼ cup parmesan with Romano cheese

1 tablespoon garlic, minced

½ tablespoon salt-free seasoning blend (I used Mrs. Dash)

Salt, to taste

Pepper, to taste

BACON:

2 24-ounce packages bacon

2 tablespoons honey

BURGERS:

½ pound burger meat (I used Bo Jackson's Grand Slam Burgers)

½ pound pork chorizo

½ pound ground beef

Havarti jalapeño cheese, sliced

Cotija cheese crumbles

BUNS AND TOPPINGS:

Brioche buns

Butter

Lettuce

Jalapeños

Hot chow chow relish

Directions

1. Heat grill and heat oven to 400°F.

AVOCADO REMOULADE SAUCE:

1. In small bowl mix together mayonnaise, avocado chunky spread, horseradish mustard, hot sauce, minced garlic, jalapeño juice, and taco seasoning.
2. Combine well and chill until ready to use.

AVOCADO CRISPY CHIPS:

1. Mix chunky avocado spread, parmesan cheese, parmesan cheese with Romano, minced garlic, seasoning, salt, and pepper.
2. Take a heaping spoonful of mix and place on a parchment-lined cookie sheet.

3. Flatten each spoonful with rolling pin.
4. Bake at 400°F for 8–9 minutes.
5. Flip crisps and cook 2½ minutes more or until golden brown.

BACON:

1. Bake or microwave bacon slices until done.
2. Baste slices with honey.
3. Set aside until ready to build burger.

BURGERS:

1. Mix burger meat, pork chorizo, and ground beef together.
2. Form into burger patties and season as desired.
3. Place on grill and cook until preferred doneness.
4. Add cheese.

BUNS:

1. Butter and toast each bun.
2. Set aside until needed.

ASSEMBLY:

1. Bottom buttered bun
2. Spread with avocado remoulade sauce
3. Lettuce
4. Hot chow chow relish
5. Burger patty with cheese
6. Jalapeño slices
7. Bacon
8. Avocado crisp chips
9. Crumble of Cotija cheese
10. Spread buttered top bun with avocado remoulade sauce
11. Top bun
12. Serve!

"No one is born a great cook; one learns by doing."

—Julia Child

Bob Armstrong Burger

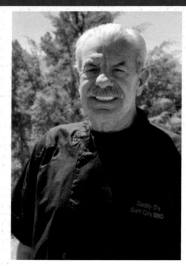

Head Cook:
Ron Otto

Team Name: Daddy O's Surf
City BBQ
Sedona, AZ

Facebook:
Daddy O's Surf City BBQ

Our burger is a take on the famous Bob Armstrong dip from Austin, Texas.

Cook Time: 1 Hour | Makes 6 servings

Ingredients

BURGERS:

2½ pounds ground chuck

2 1.25-ounce packets taco seasoning (I used Lawry's Taco Seasoning)

6 brioche buns

1 tomato, sliced

1 package nacho chips (I used Flaming Hot Doritos)

BACON:

10 slices of thick bacon

⅓ cup crushed pecans

⅓ cup brown sugar

1 teaspoon chipotle powder

HOMEMADE AVOCADO SPREAD:

3 medium avocados

2 tablespoons fresh jalapeño, diced

2 tablespoons fresh cilantro, chopped

2 tablespoons tomato, diced

2 tablespoons red onion, diced

Salt and pepper, to taste

Garlic powder, to taste

QUESO:

1 15-ounce jar of queso dip (I used 505 Green Chile Queso Dip)

1 4-ounce can diced green chilis (I used Hatch Diced Green Chilis)

Directions

1. Preheat oven to 375°F and preheat grill to medium heat.
2. Mix 2 packages of taco seasoning with 2 pounds of ground chuck. Form into 6 6-ounce patties.

BACON:

1. Arrange bacon on a cooling rack placed on top of a baking sheet.
2. Mix pecans, brown sugar, and chipotle powder in a bowl.
3. Season bacon with pecan mix and pepper.
4. Cook in a 375°F oven until bacon is crisp and the brown sugar is caramelized, about 25 minutes.
5. Cool and crumble.

HOMEMADE AVOCADO SPREAD:

1. Mix avocado with jalapeño, cilantro, tomato, red onion, salt, pepper, and garlic powder until smooth.

QUESO:

1. Mix queso dip with the diced green chilis and heat until warm.

BURGERS:

1. Cook burgers to desired temperature.
2. Toast buns.

ASSEMBLY:

1. Bottom bun
2. Avocado spread
3. Tomato slice
4. Burger patty
5. Top with queso mix
6. Sprinkle with candied bacon
7. Add 4 or 5 nacho chips
8. Spread avocado spread on top bun
9. Top burger
10. Enjoy!

"Persistence pays off."

—Ron Otto

Bull Burger

Head Cook:
Sultan Chatila

Team Name:
Tano's
Dubai, UAE

Business Name:
Tano's

Instagram:
@TanosAt8

A double thick smash three-blend burger including oxtail, brisket, and prime rib, which inspires its name: Bull Burger. Featuring a signature sauce, sliced onions, and bacon jam, plus customized, homemade Hokkaido milk buns. "Simple is King" is this burger's motto.

Prep Time: 30 Minutes | Cook Time: 45 Minutes | Makes 6 servings

Ingredients

BURGERS:
5 pounds coarse grind meat blend
6 homemade Hokkaido milk buns
12 slices premium American cheese
2 red onions, sliced

SIMPLE BACON JAM:
14 ounces bacon
2 white onions, finely chopped
⅓ cup white wine
2 tablespoons brown sugar

SPECIAL SAUCE:
2 teaspoons all-purpose seasoning (I used 2 Gringos Chupacabra Brisket Blend)
1½ cups mayonnaise
4 tablespoons ketchup
2 teaspoons sriracha
3 dill pickles, chopped

Directions

SIMPLE BACON JAM:
1. Sauté the bacon on medium heat.
2. Cook onions until caramelized in the bacon fat.
3. Add the white wine until it reduces.
4. Add the brown sugar.

SPECIAL SAUCE:
1. Make the sauce by mixing the seasoning and sauces with the chopped pickles.

BURGERS:
1. Toast the buns until they're a nicely charred, golden-brown color.
2. Put sliced onions in chilled water.
3. Heat the cast iron skillet on high heat. When it starts to smoke, smash and sear the burgers for 2 minutes on each side, adding salt to taste.
4. Put a slice of cheese on each patty, then assemble with bacon jam and special sauce.

> **TIP:**
> - You can substitute Hokkaido milk buns with French brioche buns or Hawaiian rolls.

"Good food is very often, even most often, simple food."

—Anthony Bourdain

Cajun Po' Boy Burger with Sweet Onion Cheese Sauce

A Po' Boy sandwich and cheeseburger mix with a sweet onion cheese sauce, smoked heirloom tomatoes, creole remoulade, Mache lettuce, sweet pickles, and fried shrimp.

Cook Time: 30 Minutes | Makes 4 servings

Head Cook:
Ramon Douglas

Team Name:
Burgers for Life
Altadena, CA

Facebook:
Ramon Douglas

Instagram:
@_burgersforlife_

www.BurgersForLife.com

Ingredients

CAJUN SEASONING:
(This is my own recipe, but you can buy premade)
1 tablespoon smoked paprika
2 teaspoons cayenne
1 tablespoon garlic powder
1 tablespoon oregano
1 tablespoon thyme
2 teaspoons onion powder
1 teaspoon black ground pepper
2 teaspoons salt

CREOLE REMOULADE:
2 tablespoons Cajun seasoning
1 cup mayonnaise
1 tablespoon lemon juice
1 tablespoon whole grain mustard
2 teaspoons Louisiana hot sauce

1 teaspoon Worcestershire sauce
1 tablespoon sugar

SWEET ONION CHEESE SAUCE:
2 cups sweet onions, chopped (I used Little Bear Honey Sweet Onions)
1 teaspoon minced garlic
1 tablespoon flour
2 cups Monterey Jack cheese, shredded
3 cups heavy cream
½ cup wine
1 sprig of thyme
1 sprig of oregano
Salt and pepper, to taste
1 tablespoon butter

CAJUN FRIED SHRIMP:
2 tablespoons of Cajun seasoning
12 8-12 count black tiger shrimp
2 cups flour
1 cup cornmeal
2 eggs
Oil, for frying

BURGERS:
1 pound ground beef
3 heirloom tomatoes, sliced
Sweet pickles (Any jarred sweet pickles)
Mache lettuce
4 hamburger buns (I prefer Brioche with this recipe, but you can use whatever you like)

TIP:
- You can substitute Mache lettuce with shredded Romaine or iceberg.

Directions

CAJUN SEASONING:
1. Mix together the Cajun ingredients.
2. Set aside (to be used throughout the recipe).

CREOLE REMOULADE:
1. Mix the Cajun seasoning, lemon juice, mayo, whole grain mustard, hot sauce, and Worcestershire sauce in a bowl.
2. Add salt and pepper to taste.

SWEET ONION CHEESE SAUCE:
1. Sauté the onions and garlic with the butter until translucent.

2. Add flour to make roux.
3. Add wine.
4. Cook wine down, then add thyme, oregano, and cream.
5. Once cream is hot, whisk in cheese and season with salt and pepper.

CAJUN FRIED SHRIMP:
1. Heat the oil in cast iron or deep fryer.
2. Season the shrimp with the Cajun seasoning, then dredge in flour, then egg, then in a 2-parts flour and 1-part cornmeal mixture.
3. Fry until desired temperature.

BURGERS:
1. Form ground beef into four ¼-lb patties. Season as desired and grill to preferred temperature.
2. Toast hamburger buns.
3. Build burger to your liking with all the ingredients.

"Eat responsibly."

—Ramon Douglas

Head Cook:
Tommy D'Ambrosio

Team Name:
Aioli Gourmet Burgers
Phoenix, AZ

Business Name:
Aioli Gourmet Burgers and
Catering

Facebook:
@AioliGourmet

Instagram:
@AioliGourmetBurger

www.AioliBurger.com

TIP:
• You can substitute
strawberry soda
with grenadine.

Custom burger blend (prime ribeye, short rib, chuck), pepper jack cheese, chunky avocado, bacon, chipotle aioli, sunny side egg, pickled red onions, brioche bun. This burger was created based on classic California cuisine. The creamy element from the avocado with the richness of the egg yolk paired with the acidity of the red onion play really well together with our smoky chipotle aioli. We competed with this because it is a fan favorite at our store. Being that we are located in Arizona, we have a lot of Cali lovers that dine with us and they want a taste of home.

Cook Time: 30 Minutes | Makes 4 servings

Ingredients

CHIPOTLE AIOLI:

1 tablespoon Dijon mustard

1 egg yolk

½ tablespoon tabasco sauce

1 tablespoon Worcestershire sauce

3 cloves fresh garlic, minced

1 teaspoon kosher salt

1 cup chipotles in adobo

½ cup canola oil

PICKLED RED ONIONS:

1 red onion

½ cup red wine vinegar

½ cup strawberry soda

2 tablespoons pickling spice

½ cup sugar

BURGERS:

4 8-ounce patties of custom burger blend (prime ribeye, short rib, chuck)

4 slices pepper jack cheese

8 slices bacon

4 eggs

Pinch kosher salt and peppercorn blend

4 brioche buns

Directions

1. Form burger into 8-ounce patties and season liberally to coat with kosher salt, and peppercorn blend.

2. **Make chipotle aioli:**

3. Mix Dijon mustard, egg yolk, tabasco, Worcestershire sauce, minced garlic, kosher salt, and ½ can chipotle chiles. Slowly add canola oil until emulsified.

4. **Make pickled red onions:**

5. In a sauce pot, add strawberry soda, red wine vinegar, sugar, and pickling spice and heat until it reaches a boil. Shave red onions, strain, and pour pickling liquid over onions.

6. Cook egg sunny side up.

7. Cook bacon.

8. Cook burger to desired temperature and melt cheese on top.

9. Toast bun.

ASSEMBLY:

1. Bottom bun

2. Burger with cheese

3. Bacon

4. Chunky avocado

5. 1 tablespoon chipotle aioli

6. Egg

7. 1 tablespoon chipotle aioli

8. Pickled red onion

9. Top bun

"No matter if you win or lose, competing is about pushing yourself and learning new things. As long as you're learning, you are winning. Food is life, so revel in it!"

—Tommy D'Ambrosio

Cheesy Meatless Wonder Burger

Head Cook:
Dan Hodgins

Team Name:
Chicken Chokers BBQ
Fair Lawn, NJ

Facebook:
Chicken Chokers BBQ
www.ChickenChokersBar-B-Que.com

My inspiration for this recipe was to create a burger without meat that people would enjoy just as much as a burger with meat. This is a cheesy, meatless wonder burger with a 5-cheese beer sauce, beer battered onion strips, beer fried mushrooms, fig chutney, and beer aioli.

Cook Time: 1 Hour, 30 Minutes | Makes 6 servings

Ingredients

BURGERS:

2 packages of plant-based meat (I used Impossible Meat)

4 teaspoons American Saison ale

6½ teaspoons steak seasoning (I used C+C Steak and Burger Seasoning)

4 ounces Gouda cheese, cubed

8 teaspoons BBQ sauce (I used John Boy & Billy)

Butter lettuce

Havarti cheese slices, 1 per burger

Gouda cheese slices, 1 per burger

1 3.17-ounce tube fig chutney and balsamic vinegar (I used Maison Riviere Fig Chutney & Balsamic Vinegar)

6 pretzel buns

5-CHEESE BEER SAUCE:

3 tablespoons butter

3 tablespoons flour

½ cup American Saison ale

½ cup milk

½ cup heavy cream

1 teaspoon Dijon mustard

½ teaspoon burger seasoning

½ teaspoon salt

¼ teaspoon pepper

¼ teaspoon smoked paprika

½ teaspoon onion powder

⅛ teaspoon cayenne

2 ounces Gouda cheese, shredded

2 ounces Colby cheese, shredded

2 ounces Havarti cheese, shredded

2 ounces Comté cheese, shredded

2 ounces medium cheddar cheese, shredded

BEER AIOLI:

½ cup mayonnaise

2 tablespoons Saison ale

1 teaspoon lime zest

¼ teaspoon cayenne

2¼ teaspoon smoked paprika

⅛ teaspoon garlic

2 tablespoons caramelized onion mustard

BEER MUSHROOMS:

4–6 shiitake mushrooms, sliced

6–8 baby Bella mushrooms, sliced

2 tablespoons butter

2 ounces American Saison ale

BEER-BATTERED ONION STRAWS:

1 large onion, thinly sliced

½ cup flour

½ teaspoon baking powder

1 teaspoon salt

6 ounces American Saison ale

1 large egg

1 bottle canola oil

TIP:

• You can substitute an American Saison ale with a farmhouse ale or a Belgian ale.

Directions

BURGERS:

1. Mix together small cubes of Gouda cheese, beer, seasoning, BBQ sauce, and meat.
2. Combine well and form into 6 patties.
3. Grill until done (160°F).

5-CHEESE BEER SAUCE:

1. Sauté pan over medium heat.
2. Melt butter and add flour. Whisk to combine and cook 30 seconds.
3. Add beer and whisk continuously as you pour. Eliminate any lumps.
4. Slowly add milk and cream and whisk as you pour.
5. Cook over medium heat until thick.
6. Stir in mustard, burger seasoning, salt, pepper, cayenne, and paprika. Whisk to combine.
7. Add cheese a little bit at a time.
8. Stir until completely melted.

BEER AIOLI:

1. Mix all ingredients: mayonnaise, beer, lime zest, cayenne, smoked paprika, garlic, and caramelized onion mustard.
2. Stir to combine.

BEER MUSHROOMS:

1. Melt butter in a frying pan.
2. Sauté mushrooms.
3. Deglaze pan with beer.

BEER-BATTERED ONION STRAWS:

1. Mix beer, flour, egg, baking powder, and salt in large mixing bowl. Whisk until smooth.
2. Heat oil in a large pot to 350°F–375°F.
3. Dip thin sliced onions in batter, then fry for 3 minutes until golden brown.
4. Transfer to paper-lined plate.
5. Repeat in small batches to avoid clumping.

DIRECTIONS CONTINUED

ASSEMBLY:

1. Bottom bun
2. Lettuce
3. Drizzle beer aioli over lettuce
4. Burger
5. Beer mushrooms
6. Cheese slices (1 each of Havarti and Gouda)
7. Generous amount of 5-cheese beer sauce
8. Top with onion straws
9. Smear fig chutney on the inside of top bun
10. Place top bun on burger

"Recipes have heart. You must bring the soul. Follow your heart. Season with love. Enjoy!"

—Dan Hodgins

Chimi-Chorizo Burger

Our recipe includes ⁵⁰/₅₀ pork and Texan Wagyu beef chorizo, fresh chimichurri, griddled mozza, honey butter, onion tanglers, and smoked chili lime mayo on a brioche bun. This burger came to fruition from a lengthy thought process as we advanced into the second round of the World Food Championships. To be completely honest, we sat in our hotel room in south Dallas, overlooking our leaf-covered drained pool while listening to re-runs on the TV and doing our laundry.

Once we had advanced to the second round, we knew we had to come up with a burger that would be just as satisfying as the first. Our culinary backgrounds, paired with our educational experience, allowed us to envision a burger that felt most comfortable and met the contest requirements. Inspiration came from the utilization of the 2 Gringos Chupacabra Brisket Magic Seasoning that we felt paired as perfect seasoning within our chorizo burger, and also seasoned beautifully on our crispy onion tangles.

Head Cook:
Christopher Bunter
& Andrew Hess

Team Name:
Alberta Burger Boys
Edmonton, Alberta, CA

Business Name:
Edmonton Public Schools

Instagram:
@adlibedmonton;
@Chris.Bunter.85

Prep Time: 40–45 minutes | Cook Time: 15–20 minutes | Makes 4-6 Servings

Ingredients

CHIMICHURRI:
1 cup chopped bell pepper

1 small jalapeño (or similar), seeded and chopped

2 Roma tomatoes, chopped, salted, and water squeezed out

2 teaspoons garlic, minced

⅓ cup olive oil

¼ cup red wine vinegar

1 teaspoon dried oregano

1 tablespoon paprika

1 teaspoon salt

1 bunch parsley, chopped

ONION TANGLERS:
2–3 small onions, sliced into thin rings

1½ cups buttermilk

3 tablespoons of brisket rub seasoning, divided (we used 2 Gringos Chupacabra Brisket Magic, or any seasoning of your choice)

1½ cups flour

1½ cups cornstarch

2½ liters vegetable oil for frying

SMOKED MAYO:
1 cup mayonnaise

⅛ teaspoon cayenne pepper

2 teaspoons paprika

Zest of 2 limes

½ teaspoon of liquid smoke*
(see note)

HONEY BUTTER:
½ cup butter, softened

⅓ cup honey

chili powder, to taste

BURGERS:
1 pound coarse ground pork

1 pound coarse ground Wagyu beef flank (or any beef that you prefer, but a little more fat is preferred)

3 tablespoons paprika

3 tablespoons brisket rub seasoning (we used 2 Gringos Chupacabra Brisket Magic, or any seasoning of your choice)

1 teaspoon minced garlic

¼ cup apple cider vinegar

12 skim milk mozzarella cheese slices

6 brioche burger buns

Directions

CHIMICHURRI:
1. Make sure all the fresh ingredients are washed well and cleaned before preparing.
2. Add all the ingredients into a food processor, not a blender. Make sure to only pulse the mixture. (It should not be puréed!)
3. Season to taste. (Will keep up to 1 week in the fridge.)

ONION TANGLERS:
1. Peel and slice onions on a mandolin into rings (⅛-inch wide). If you have access to a slicer or mandolin, it will yield nicer results.
2. Soak for at least 30 minutes in buttermilk.
3. Mix flour and cornstarch together and half of the brisket rub seasoning.
4. Heat oil in a deep pot or a deep fryer if you have one (it works well and is a safer option).

5. When ready to fry, drain onions in a colander and then dredge in the flour and cornstarch mixture. Shake off excess flour and fry at 350°F until crispy.
6. Lift out of fryer and place on a plate lined with paper towels to wick away excess grease.
7. Season with salt and remaining brisket rub seasoning as desired.

"Trust your instincts, practicing 15 times is not necessarily better than practicing three times. Create a detailed and timed work plan. Follow it. It takes the guess work out of competition day. Trust your team. They have your back. Taste everything. Have fun."

—**Christopher Bunter & Andrew Hess**

DIRECTIONS CONTINUED

SMOKED MAYO:

1. Measure the mayo and put into a mixing bowl.

2. Add cayenne, lime zest, and paprika. Mix together until evenly distributed.

3. Place in a large resealable plastic bag and inflate using a smoking gun (applewood or cherry chips). Allow smoke to infuse for at least 30–40 minutes.

*Note: We used a handheld smoking gun for the smoke flavor. If you don't have one, add ½ teaspoon liquid smoke.

HONEY BUTTER:

1. Measure out softened butter.

2. Add honey and mix together.

3. Season with chili powder to desired taste

4. Keep softened and set aside.

BURGERS:

1. Measure ingredients, leaving the pork and beef in the fridge until the last minute.

2. Bring out meat and combine in a large mixing bowl with the other ingredients and half of the brisket seasoning.

3. Round by hand until emulsified and then divide into 6 equal portions for smashing on grill.

4. Heat griddle to 500°F. Smash meat on griddle and allow to crust. Season with remaining brisket seasoning. Cook 2–3 minutes and then flip once the crust has formed.

5. Cook until the internal temperature is 165°F. Brush with honey butter on top.

ASSEMBLY:

1. Once sauces are made, onions are crisp, and burgers are grilled, toast the buns in a hot oven for 3–4 minutes. Brush with honey butter if desired.

2. In a large frying pan, sear sliced mozzarella cheese on squares of oiled parchment paper. When the bottom side is thoroughly browned, turn carefully onto each burger.

Once the cheese is on the burger, peel off the parchment carefully to leave the cheese on the burger in place.

3. Assemble burgers starting with chimichurri on the bottom, then burgers with honey butter glaze, followed by griddled mozzarella, and onion tanglers. Spread smoked chili mayo on the top bun. Carefully place the top bun on the Chimi-Chorizo Burger and serve.

Chunky Guacamole Cheeseburger with Candied Bacon

Going into the final round of the 2018 World Burger Competition, we hadn't really thought this recipe through because, well, it's hard to make the Top Ten. The competition is extremely tough because everyone is a winner. They didn't just show up and compete. They had to win their way into the World Food Championships. We were in 8th place, and we were simply excited be a finalist. We knew chunky avocado was the required infused ingredient, and it had to be one fabulous burger to propel us to World Champions. So, the night before the final round, the KirbyG's® crew set about to creating a guacamole recipe that subtly packed a wallop of flavors. The results were astounding! We jumped from 8th place to first with one of the largest point changes in WFC history. Our recipe featured a Bo's Angus Beef Burger topped with pepper jack Havarti cheese, candied bacon, and chunky guacamole. We added a lime avocado aioli for the perfect mixture of sweet, sour, spicy and savory.

Head Cook:
Neil Daniell

Team Name:
KirbyG's Diner
McDonough, GA

Business Name:
KirbyG's Diner

Facebook:
KirbyG's Diner

Instagram:
@KirbyGsDiner

Twitter:
@KirbyGsDiner

www.KirbyGs.com

Prep Time: 45 Minutes | Cook Time: 15 Minutes | Makes 5 servings

Ingredients

BURGERS:

5 slices pepper jack Havarti cheese

5 buns, buttered and toasted; approximately 4" diameter

5 ea. ½ lb. Angus beef patties (I used Bo's Angus Beef Burger patties)

Seasoning, to taste (Note: I used a steak rub of equal parts garlic powder, salt, and fine ground pepper.)

AVOCADO AIOLI:

¼ cup olive oil mayonnaise

½ cup chunky avocado spread

2 tablespoons lime juice

1 tablespoon fajita seasoning

1 tablespoon fresh cracked pepper

½ cup guacamole (I used Sabra)

CHUNKY GUACAMOLE:

3 avocados, peeled and diced

¼ cup onion (red and/or white)

2 medium Roma tomatoes, diced

1 tablespoon jalapeño, seeded and finely chopped

2 tablespoons cilantro, diced

2 tablespoons lime juice

Salt and pepper, to taste

CANDIED BACON:

1 pound sliced bacon

1 cup pure maple syrup

1 cup brown sugar

2 teaspoons red pepper flakes

1 teaspoon paprika

1 teaspoon chili powder

1 teaspoon Cajun seasoning (I used Slap Ya Mama Hot Cajun Seasoning)

¼ teaspoon onion powder

¼ teaspoon garlic powder

¼ teaspoon pepper

GARNISH: (Optional)

½ cup of tri-color tortilla strips

TIP:
- You can substitute the avocado spread with 1 cup of guacamole.

Directions

CANDIED BACON:

1. Preheat oven to 350°F.
2. Whisk together the syrup and dry ingredients to make candied bacon topping.
3. Line a baking pan with parchment paper. Lay out your bacon on the lined pan.
4. Brush the syrup mixture onto both sides of the bacon for best results.
5. Bake for approximately 20 minutes total at 350°F. The time will vary depending on elevation and oven type.
6. At approximately the 10-minute mark, you will flip the bacon over and cook the opposite side.
7. Around the 15–18-minute mark, you should begin to watch the candied bacon closely because it burns easily. You want the bacon to look brown and somewhat pliable. It may even look slightly undercooked. However, it will firm up nicely after it cools. If it's dark and crispy, you've cooked it too long and the sugars will taste burnt.
8. Once you remove the bacon from the oven, place the candied bacon strips immediately place on cooling racks.

AVOCADO AIOLI AND CHUNKY GUACAMOLE:

1. While bacon is cooking/cooling, prepare the aioli and guacamole using the ingredients above.
2. Once complete, lightly butter and toast buns to golden brown. (Note: I recommend using butter on the top bun only to prevent sogginess.)

BURGERS:

1. Preheat pan/grill to 400°F.
2. Season outside of patty to taste. Using my steak rub or something equivalent.

"It takes a master to bring all these flavors together and make it pop. The key is using the five senses of taste—salty, sweet, spicy, sour, and savory (umami). Use each in moderation so they don't overpower each other. Too spicy, you will actually turn people off. Too sweet, and you can't taste the sourness of the lime. So, be subtle as you craft your dish."

—Neil Daniell

DIRECTIONS CONTINUED

3. Cook the burger patties to your desired temperature. ServSafe recommends 155°F, which is medium-well.

4. Top each patty with 1 slice of pepper jack Havarti when the patty is approximately 10 degrees below your desired final temp. Melt cheese. (Note: A spritz of water will help it melt faster.)

ASSEMBLY:

1. Bottom bun (toasted, no butter)

2. 1 tablespoon avocado aioli

3. Burger patty with melted cheese

4. 2 slices candied bacon; place in X pattern

5. ¼–½ cup chunky guacamole

6. Top bun (toasted, with butter)

7. Optional: Garnish plate with tri-color tortilla strips to make a colorful presentation

A spicy, cheese-stuffed cowboy burger infused with jalapeños, and stacked with spicy cheese, applewood smoked bacon, lettuce, barbecue sauce, and fried onion petals on a toasted brioche bun!

Cook Time: 45 Minutes | Makes 12 servings

Head Cook:
Suzanne Burton

Team Name:
Hot, Thick & Juicy
Madison, AL

Ingredients

FRIED ONION PETALS:

1 large onion (I used Little Bear Produce Honey Sweet Onion)

1¾ cups self-rising flour

1½ cups buttermilk

Salt and pepper, to taste

Seasoned salt, to taste

Crisco oil for frying

BURGERS:

24 strips bacon, cooked (I used Wright Brand Applewood Smoked Bacon)

12 brioche buns, toasted

⅔ stick butter (I used Challenge Salted Butter)

1½ teaspoon garlic powder

12 burger patties (5.33 ounces each) (I used Bo Jackson Burger Patties)

12 ounces Wagyu ground beef ($^{80}/_{20}$)

6 jalapeños, grated

1 tablespoon BBQ seasoning (I used Rebel Rub)

1 tablespoon all-purpose seasoning (I used Boar's Night Out White Lightning, plus extra for seasoning the outside of the patty)

1 tablespoon steak seasoning (I used Killer Hogs Steak Rub, plus extra for seasoning the outside of the patty)

24 pepper jack cracker cuts + 12 slices pepper jack cheese

12 pieces green leaf lettuce

12 slices tomato, with salt and pepper

24 dill pickle slices

14 ounces BBQ sauce, for topping (I used Sonny's Sweet BBQ Sauce)

12 multi-colored cherry tomatoes, for topping

12 baby dill pickles, for topping

Duck fat spray

TIPS:

- You can substitute Wagyu ground beef with ground top ribeye steak or any other ground heavily marbled meat with a high fat content.

- You can substitute duck fat with canola oil or other oil spray.

Directions

1. **Make the bacon:**
2. Render the bacon in a pan over medium heat until crispy; set aside on paper towels.
3. **Make the buns:**
4. Melt ⅔ stick of butter in a microwave-safe bowl. With a brush, baste the inside of the bun with butter and sprinkle each half lightly with garlic powder. Toast the inside of the buns in a skillet over medium heat.

FRIED ONION PETALS:

1. Slice one large onion into medium slices and cut into petals.
2. Soak in buttermilk and dredge in seasoned self-rising flour.
3. Fry the onion petals until they are golden brown and puffed, about 3 minutes per batch.

4. Drain on paper towels and season lightly with seasoned salt.
5. Repeat with the remaining onion rings and batter; serve hot.

BURGERS:

1. Preheat a gas grill to high heat and coat the grates with duck fat spray.
2. Combine the burger patties, wagyu ground beef, grated jalapeños, and seasonings in a large bowl.
3. Mix with your hands until just combined.
4. Form 12 burger patties and stuff with 2 slices of pepper jack cracker cuts per patty.
5. Lightly sprinkle with all-purpose and steak seasonings on both sides of the patty.

6. Cook until the burger reaches an internal temperature of 155°F.
7. Just before you remove it from the grill, put a piece of pepper jack cheese on top. Then remove from heat and let rest for 10 minutes.

ASSEMBLY:

1. Dress both sides of each bun with BBQ Sauce.
2. Place a piece of green leaf lettuce on the bottom bun and top with 1 slice of tomato (salt and pepper to taste).
3. Next, place a burger patty with 1 slice of pepper jack cheese, and top with 2 dill pickle slices.
4. Lay 2 strips of bacon crossed.
5. Top with fried onion petals.
6. Place the top bun on each burger.

"Cooking well doesn't mean cooking fancy."
—Julia Child

Country Fried Thanksgiving Impossible Burger

A Tank 7 beer battered Impossible burger patty, Impossible sausage and onion gravy, cranberry sauce, and Saison sausage stuffing made with Impossible sausage and Boulevard Tank 7 Saison.

Head Cook:
David Calkins

Team Name:
Burger Republic
Nashville, TN

Facebook:
Burger Republic

Instagram:
@Burger_Republic

www.BurgerRepublic.com

Cook Time: 1 Hour | Makes 6 servings

Ingredients

BEER BATTER:

12 ounces beer (I used Boulevard Tank 7 Saison)

6 eggs

1 quart buttermilk

4 cups flour, divided

2 cups potato starch

2 cups chicken fry

SAISON SAUSAGE STUFFING (IMPOSSIBLE):

1 sweet onion, chopped

6 ribs celery, chopped

1 head garlic, minced

1 quart vegetable stock

1 pound plant-based spicy sausage (I used Impossible Spicy Sausage)

12 ounces beer (I used Boulevard Tank 7 Saison)

1 teaspoon vegetable bouillon (I used Better Than Bouillon Vegetable)

¼ cup butter

24 ounces stuffing mix (I used Pepperidge Farm)

1 teaspoon poultry seasoning

1 teaspoon onion powder

1 teaspoon garlic powder

IMPOSSIBLE SAISON COUNTRY GRAVY:

1 onion, chopped

½ cup butter

½ cup flour

12 ounces beer (I used Boulevard Tank 7 Saison)

1 quart vegetable stock

1 teaspoon onion bouillon

1 quart heavy cream

1 teaspoon poultry seasoning (vegetarian)

1 teaspoon garlic powder

1 teaspoon onion powder

½ teaspoon black pepper

1 teaspoon rosemary, chopped

1 pound plant-based sausage (I used Impossible Sausage)

12 4-ounce plant-based burger patties (I used Impossible Burger Patties)

12 brioche buns

1 gallon peanut oil

28 ounces cranberry sauce (I used Ocean Spray Whole Cranberry Sauce)

2 cups English peas

TIP:

- You can substitute potato starch with cornstarch.

Directions

BEER BATTER:

1. Hand form 6 4-ounce patties and set aside.
2. Combine all ingredients (excluding 2 cups of flour) in bowl and stir until batter is smooth.
3. Place remaining flour in separate bowl.
4. Bread burgers by coating with flour, covering evenly in batter and again in flour. Set aside.
5. Preheat oil to 375°F.
6. Place burgers separately in hot oil for 1 minute each. Set aside on baking sheet.

SAISON SAUSAGE STUFFING (IMPOSSIBLE):

1. In large stock pot, sauté onion and celery and garlic.
2. Add sausage and brown in pan for 5 minutes.
3. Add remaining ingredients (excluding stuffing mix).
4. Simmer for 5 minutes.
5. Add stuffing mix and transfer to buttered baking sheet. Bake for 30 minutes at 350°F.

IMPOSSIBLE SAISON COUNTRY GRAVY:

1. In a medium saucepan, melt butter and sauté onions until tender.
2. Add flour to make roux. Cook for 1 minute on medium heat.
3. Add Saison and vegetable stock. Simmer for 5 minutes.
4. Add remaining ingredients. Simmer for 5 minutes.

ASSEMBLY:

1. Butter and toast brioche buns.
2. Cover inside of bottom bun evenly with cranberry sauce.
3. Add patty and lightly cover with 2 ounces Saison country gravy.
4. Add 4 ounces Saison sausage stuffing.
5. Cover inside of top bun with 2 ounces Saison country gravy and English peas.

"Cooking is about passion, so it may look slightly temperamental in a way that it's too assertive to the naked eye."

—Gordon Ramsay

Fiesta Street Corn Burger

Head Cook:
Joseph Martinez

Team Name:
Team Tributary
San Antonio, TX

Business Name:
Marriott Rivercenter on the
Riverwalk, Tributary Restaurant

Instagram:
@JosephThadeus_Cooks

www.TributarySA.com

Growing up, Elote was a snack I would crave on the weekends as I shopped the outdoor markets with my family. The flavors balance perfectly with the sweetness of the corn and the acidity of the chili and lime. Combined with Texas beef, chicharrons, locally made chorizo, and a Cotija/Oaxaca cheese whiz. This burger shows a beautiful merging of Texas and Mexican culture and products. My absolute favorite component in this recipe is the Oaxaca cheese whiz. The texture of the cheese when melted is everything you would want from melted cheese and it can be added to pretty much anything!

Prep Time: 45 Minutes | Cook Time: 20 Minutes | Makes 6 servings

Ingredients

STREET CORN:

2 links chorizo

1 tablespoon butter

4 cups corn, removed from cobs

1 cup diced bell peppers

4 ounces lime juice

1 cup cilantro, chopped

1 ounce dried chilis

1 cup mayonnaise

1 tablespoon seasoning (I used Chupacabra Special Blend Seasoning)

Cooking oil, as needed

CHICHARRON CORN NUT CRUNCH:

1 cup chicharron, uncooked

1 tablespoon all-purpose seasoning (I used Chupacabra Chop House Blend Seasoning)

1 cup corn nuts

Cooking oil

OAXACA CHEESE WHIZ:

3 garlic cloves, roasted

1 quart heavy cream

½ cup Oaxaca cheese

½ cup Cotija cheese

1 teaspoon xanthan gum

BURGERS:

6 4-ounce burger patties

Garlic oil

6 sourdough buns

TIPS:

- You can substitute chicharron with chicken skin or bacon. (It won't taste exactly the same, but will work fine if in a pinch.)

- You can substitute xanthan gum with cornstarch.

Directions

STREET CORN:

1. In a large skillet, cook the chorizo and render until fully cooked. Remove from pan and set aside.

2. Add 1 tablespoon of butter to pan and add corn and peppers. Sauté for 3 minutes in chorizo fat and butter. Remove from heat and allow to cool.

3. Once cooked, combine in bowl with lime juice, chopped cilantro, dried chilis, and mayonnaise.

4. Add chorizo into the street corn mix. Season to taste.

CHICHARRON CORN NUT CRUNCH:

1. Preheat oil in pan to 400°F.

2. Drop uncooked chicharron in oil and submerge until cooked and puffy.

3. Remove from heat into mixing bowl and immediately toss with seasoning. Allow to cool.

4. In food processor, combine chicharron and corn nuts and pulse until the corn nuts are in small pieces.

5. Remove from processor and toss in mixing bowl with more seasoning to taste.

OAXACA CHEESE WHIZ:

1. Roast garlic in oven at 350°F for 10 minutes until soft.

2. In medium-sized sauce pot, heat heavy cream to 190°F.

3. Remove from heat and add to blender. Add 1 cup of shredded Oaxaca cheese and roasted garlic, and blend until smooth.

4. Add cup of shredded Cotija cheese to thicken up. Add 1 teaspoon of xanthan gum to stabilize and keep blending until ingredients are fully incorporated. Allow to cool.

5. When cooled, put in a canister and charge with 1 tank. Set aside.

BURGERS:

1. Brush buns with garlic oil. Toast in oven at 350°F for 3 minutes until golden.

2. In a cast iron skillet, sear patties over medium-high heat for 3 minutes on one side until crust begins to form. Then flip the patties and cook an additional 2 minutes and top patties with Oaxaca cheese whiz, then cover for final minute to melt cheese. Remove from heat.

ASSEMBLY:

1. Begin building burger by laying out toasted bottom bun.

2. Place patty on top of bun.

3. Lay street corn generously on top of melted cheese whiz.

4. Cover with chicharron corn nut crunch and top bun.

5. Enjoy!

"Food is truly the one thing in the world that can create joy and bring people together. Growing up, food was always the reason our family would come together. To this day, my absolute favorite moments in life are the times I am surrounded by great company and great food."

—Joseph Martinez

Fried Pimento Cheeseburger

Head Cooks:
Drew Jackman & David Calkins

Team Name:
Burger Republic
Nashville, TN

Business Name:
Burger Republic

Facebook:
Burger Republic

Instagram:
@Burger_Republic

www.BurgerRepublic.com

A beef patty topped with fried pimento cheese, honey sweet onion jam, soda-glazed bacon, horseradish remoulade, and Texas pickles.

Cook Time: 45 Minutes | Makes 12 servings

Ingredients

BURGERS:
½ pound 80% beef patty (I used Bo Jackson's Beef)
½ pound 20% proprietary meat blend
Salt and pepper, to taste
2 cups Texas pickles (for topping)

ONION JAM:
1 cup honey whiskey (I used Jack Daniel's Tennessee Honey Whiskey)
½ cup vinegar

1 cup hoisin
¼ cup brown sugar
2 cups sweet onions, chopped

SODA-GLAZED BACON:
1 cup soda (I used Dr. Pepper)
2 pounds bacon (I used Benton's Bacon)
Honey whiskey glaze (reserved from Onion Jam recipe below)

HORSERADISH REMOULADE:
2 cups mayonnaise

1 cup ketchup
¼ cup horseradish

PIMENTO CHEESE PATTIES:
2 pounds pimento cheese
3 cups flour
6 eggs
4 cups panko breadcrumbs

BUNS:
12 brioche rolls
1 pound butter

Directions

BURGER PATTIES:
1. Combine 80% Bo's Grand Slam Patty with 20% proprietary blend beef. Portion to 6 ounces per burger and season with salt and pepper. Set aside.

ONION JAM:
1. Combine honey whiskey, vinegar, hoisin sauce, and brown sugar. Cook until thick.
2. Set half of mixture aside for bacon glaze.
3. Caramelize onions in a stock pot and simmer until sweet and tender.
4. Add half of honey whiskey glaze to onions. Set aside.

SODA-GLAZED BACON:
1. Take half of honey whiskey glaze and add soda.
2. Dip each piece of bacon into glaze and bake for 15 minutes. Set aside.

HORSERADISH REMOULADE:
1. Combine mayonnaise, ketchup, and horseradish. Set aside.

PIMENTO CHEESE PATTIES:
1. Make 2-ounce cheese patties and coat in flour.
2. Dip in egg wash, then in panko breadcrumbs. Set aside.

BRIOCHE ROLLS:
1. Melt butter and brush both sides of the rolls with the butter and toast on flat top until golden.

ASSEMBLY:
1. Cook burger to medium degree of doneness, place on bottom bun, top with 1 tablespoon onion jam.
2. Cook pimento cheese patties in 350°F-oil for 30 seconds. Drain oil and place on top of burger patty with onion jam.
3. Top with soda-glazed bacon and pickles.
4. Smear top bun with horseradish remoulade and place on top of pickles.
5. Eat!

"*Food is our common ground, a universal experience.*"

—James Beard

Head Cook:
Jose Perrotta

Team Name:
El Camion
Santo Domingo D.N.,
Dominican Republic

Business Name:
El Camión

Instagram:
@ElCamionRD
and @ChefJG.Perrottas

This recipe is focused on our infused ingredient, honey sweet onions (Little Bear Produce), used in different ways and textures in our burger. The inspiration is recreating a well-known traditional French dish, French onion soup. The burger is structured with beef patties, stuffed with onion jam and goat cheese, onion soup cream, stuffed onion ring with truffled mushroom and bacon duxelles, and gratin Swiss cheese.

Cook Time: 45 Minutes | Makes 11 servings

Ingredients

GOAT CHEESE ONION JAM:

4 large yellow onions, julienne cut

1 teaspoon salt

½ teaspoon black pepper

1 cup granulated cane sugar

10 ounces goat cheese

BEEF PATTIES:

11 pretzel buns

5 pounds ground beef
(your selection)

3 tablespoons liquid smoke

Salt, to taste

Pepper, to taste

1 tablespoon granulated garlic

1 tablespoon granulated onion

ONION SOUP CREAM:

5 large yellow onions, julienne cut

1 liter beef stock

1 pint heavy cream

Salt and pepper, to taste

STUFFED ONION RINGS:

1 tablespoon butter

1 large yellow onion

3½ pounds mushrooms, minced

4 tablespoons cream cheese

4 ounces bacon, cooked
and chopped

1 tablespoon truffle oil

1 pound all-purpose flour

4 large eggs, beaten

1 pound panko breadcrumbs

Salt and pepper, to taste

1 quart vegetable oil

REMAINING INGREDIENTS

8 ounces butter

5 ounces bacon

8 ounces cream cheese

½ pound grated parmesan cheese

Directions

GOAT CHEESE ONION JAM:

1. Preheat pan, add onions, and cook until golden brown.

2. Add 1 teaspoon of salt and ½ teaspoon of black pepper and let cook for 2–3 minutes more on medium heat.

3. Add sugar until fully caramelized.

4. Let it rest for about 8 minutes in refrigerator and then mix with goat cheese to stuff patties.

BEEF PATTIES:

1. Add ground beef to bowl, add liquid smoke, and mix well.

2. Set in refrigerator until use.

3. In a small bowl, mix 60% salt, 20% black pepper, 10% granulated garlic, and 10% granulated onion for seasoning.

ONION SOUP CREAM:

1. Preheat pan, add onions, and cook until golden brown.

2. Add beef stock, season to taste, and cook until reduction.

3. Add 1 pint of heavy cream, let cook for 3 minutes on medium heat, then process in blender.

4. Take cream back to pan, let it reduce and season to taste.

STUFFED ONION RINGS:

1. Preheat pan and add butter.

2. Add mushrooms to pan and cook until golden brown.

3. Add salt and pepper to taste and let cook until dry.

4. Remove from pan into a bowl and add cream cheese, crunchy bacon bites, and truffle oil and mix. Let it cool.

5. Take the onion and cut into rings. Fill it with the mushroom mixture and let it rest in the freezer or refrigerator until firm, 20 minutes.

6. For the breading process, dust the onion rings in plain flour, then dip in beaten eggs and bread with panko breadcrumbs. Fry the stuffed onion rings until golden brown.

ASSEMBLY:

1. Season patties with seasoning mix to taste, take to grill, and cook until desired temperature (recommended: medium-well).

2. Toast buns in oven for 4–5 minutes at 400°F. Take toasted bun to plate, add cooked patty, top with onion soup cream, then Swiss cheese and gratin, and fried stuffed onion ring.

3. Top with another slice of Swiss cheese and gratin, complete with the top bun, and serve.

"*Laughter is brightest where food is best.*"

—Irish Proverb

Loaded Riviera Deluxe

Head Cook:
Travis Moody

Team Name:
Travis Moody
Middlesboro, KY

Facebook:
Travis Moody

Instagram:
@LaughAtTrav

This is a pepper jack-filled burger, sitting on a layer of sautéed kale and bacon, then topped with guacamole, fried tomatillo, and drunken red onion, for a flavor to explode in your mouth! We had to use the guacamole as a key ingredient, so I wanted to put a southern spin on the burger, yet keep it in the southwest category, so I took a tomatillo in place of a green tomato, used some kale for some more southern roots, you can't leave out the bacon…then I juiced up some onions in some whiskey and sautéed them.

Cook Time: 30–45 Minutes | Makes 6 servings

Ingredients

6 5.3-ounce burger patties

1½–2 tablespoons homemade guacamole (recipe below)

8 ounces chunky avocado

2 ounces pimento

1 clove garlic, minced

8 strips bacon

4 cups kale

1 red onion, sliced

½ stick butter, melted

½ cup whiskey (I used Redneck Riviera Whiskey)

1 tomatillo, sliced

1 cup flour

1 cup corn meal

1 large egg

Salt

Pepper

Brioche buns (I used Bo Jackson's Pina Colada Brioche Bun)

Vegetable oil

Lime

Directions

1. Preheat grill to 425°F.
2. **Make quick guacamole:**
3. Combine avocado with pimentos and garlic. Squeeze ½ lime juice. Season with salt and pepper to taste.
4. Stuff burger patty with pepper jack cheese, then season with salt and pepper.
5. Fry 8 strips of bacon, then set to the side. Reserve grease for kale.
6. Chop kale and sauté in bacon grease 5–8 minutes on medium-high heat.
7. Brush onions with oil. Grill until soft, transfer to sauté pan with ½ stick melted butter on medium-high heat for another 5 minutes. Add whiskey and flambé.
8. Dip tomatillos in flour/cornmeal mix (seasoned with salt and pepper), then dredge in egg wash and fry in oil.
9. Grill burgers until internal temperature of 155°F.
10. To build the burger, start with bun base, topped with kale, then bacon, followed with burger, topped with guacamole, tomatillo, onions, then top bun.

"I've always enjoyed cooking for others. I like to see their reactions to what I prepare for them. When you cook with love, people can tell a difference."

—Travis Moody

Head Cook:
Hiram Quintana

Team Name:
Sizzle
Pottstown, PA

Instagram:
@Chef_Hiram_Quintana

Southwest chili cheeseburger with a stuffed Impossible patty layered with southwest flavors to create a southwestern nacho experience while enjoying an amazing, plant-based burger!

Cook Time: 45 Minutes | Makes 4–6 servings

Ingredients

Brioche rolls

3 pounds plant-based meat (I used Impossible Meat)

1 head iceberg lettuce

3 pounds heirloom tomatoes

1 cup oak-smoked olive oil

6 cloves black garlic

2 cups cilantro, finely chopped

3 pounds Spanish onions, thinly sliced

3 limes

4 large jalapeños, roasted and minced

2½ pounds aged cheddar cheese

2 12-ounce cans black beans

1 pound red bell peppers

1 bag tri-colored tortilla chips

1 cup tomato paste

2 cups petite tomatoes

1 cup diced tomatoes

1 cup tomato love (I used Red Gold)

1 cup all-purpose flour

1 4-ounce bag chips (I used Doritos)

1 pound butter

Zest of 2 lemons

1 12-ounce can beer (I used Tank 7 American Saison)

Southwest spice seasoning, to taste

2 quarts vegetable oil

Salt and pepper, to taste

1 cup heavy cream

1 avocado

Directions

1. Combine butter, 6 cloves black garlic, zest of 1 lemon and 1 tablespoons beer (I used Tank 7 American Saison). Mix then set aside.

2. Cut roll spread compound butter, then set aside.

3. Shred lettuce and mix with 1 cup cilantro, zest of 1 lemon, oak-smoked olive oil, and salt and pepper to taste. Set aside.

4. Slice heirloom tomatoes and season with oak smoked olive oil, citrus, and southwest rub and set aside.

5. Peel and slice avocado set aside.

6. Take plant-based meat and combine 3 cups crushed tortilla chips, cilantro, southwest spice. Portion into 6 ounces then stuff with cheddar and black garlic. Set aside.

7. In hot pan, sauté and caramelize onions with beer and black garlic. Set aside.

8. In saucepan, reduce 2 cups beer add heavy cream. Simmer and slowly add 2 pounds chopped cheddar cheese. Simmer then add ½ cup minced roasted jalapeños. Turn down heat, then set aside.

9. Put vegetable oil in saucepan preheat to 345°F.

10. In bowl, mix onions and coat with flour and southwest dust then fry until golden brown. Set aside.

11. Place bottom of roll on plate and layer all ingredients into the brioche and enjoy.

Black Garlic Substitute Recipe

1. Roast 1 bulb of garlic.

2. Cut in half and rub with olive oil.

3. Wrap tightly in foil and bake at 350°F for 20–30 minutes.

4. Add a few drops of balsamic vinegar to the cloves when cooled.

"*There is no love sincerer than the love of food.*"

—George Bernard Shaw

Pimento Cheeseburger with Honey Sweet Onion Bacon Jam

I credit Aunt Martha for this fabulous gem. Well, the pimento cheese dip, at least. I can still hear her sweet southern drawl years ago telling me to use ranch dressing instead of mayo. The rest is history as we pulled out the stops to pack a wallop of flavors in this great burger. One bite will have you wanting more! It's topped with lettuce, tomato, fried pickles chips, salty but spicy jalapeño bacon, tangy pimento cheese, and homemade honey sweet onion bacon jam. It's placed on a soft bun to hold all these flavors together.

Prep Time: 1 Hour | Cook Time: 15 Minutes | Makes 4–6 servings

Head Cook:
Neil Daniell

Team Name:
KirbyG's Diner
McDonough, GA

Business Name:
KirbyG's Diner

Facebook:
KirbyG's Diner

Instagram:
@KirbyGsDiner

Twitter:
@KirbyGsDiner

www.KirbyGs.com

Ingredients

BURGERS:
5 buns, buttered and toasted; approximately 4" diameter

5½-pound beef burger patties

5–10 tomato slices

10 slices bacon (I used Hormel Black Label Jalapeño Bacon)

2 cups bacon jam

2½ cups pimento cheese

20 fried dill pickle chips

12-ounce package arugula or green leaf lettuce

Garlic seasoning, to taste (I use equal parts garlic powder, salt, and fine ground black pepper)

FRIED PICKLE CHIPS:
16 ounces dill pickle slices, drained and dried on paper towels

1 cup seasoned panko breadcrumbs

1 cup chicken fry breading or equivalent (I used House of Autry Chicken Fry Breading)

¾ cup buttermilk

Fajita seasoning, to taste

Vegetable oil for frying

(Note: Some panko and breading have seasoning in them. I added a steak rub of equal parts garlic powder, salt, and fine ground pepper so it had just enough flavor.)

(**Optional Note:** If you don't have time to make fried dill pickles, simply add 4–6 oz dill pickle relish to the spicy pimento cheese recipe. You will add it at the same time as the diced pimentos and jalapeños.)

SPICY PIMENTO CHEESE:
12 ounces smokey sharp cheddar, grated

12 ounces extra sharp cheddar, grated

4 ounces cream cheese, softened

4 ounces sliced pimentos, undrained

4 ounces diced jalapeños, (hot) undrained

1 teaspoon garlic powder

Cayenne pepper, to taste

¼ honey sweet onion, finely diced or grated

4–6 ounces chipotle dressing (I used Hidden Valley Ranch Southwest Chipotle Dressing)

Dash salt and pepper

Dash smoked paprika

Optional: 4–6 ounces dill pickle relish (I used Mt. Olive Simply Relish Deli Style Dill)

HONEY SWEET ONION BACON JAM:
1½ pounds jalapeño or peppered bacon; diced into 1-inch pieces

1 cup shallots, finely chopped

2 cups honey sweet onion, finely chopped

4 garlic cloves, finely chopped

1 teaspoon chili powder

½ teaspoon smoked paprika

½ cup bourbon

½ cup maple syrup

¼ cup balsamic vinegar

½ cup brown sugar

Directions

BACON:
1. You are using bacon in two different ways in this recipe, as strips and bacon jam. First, cook approximately 10 slices of jalapeño (or peppered) bacon to use as strips. Cook over medium heat until it browns perfectly. Transfer to paper towels to drain excess fat off.

HONEY SWEET ONION BACON JAM:
1. With the remainder of the bacon, prepare the bacon jam.
2. Using a sharp knife or scissors, cut the regular bacon into small, 1-inch pieces. You can also tear it by hand so it looks more rustic, but not too perfect. (Personal choice.)
3. Cook over medium heat until it browns perfectly. You will want the bacon a little crisper with as little

visible fat as possible. Transfer to paper towels to drain excess fat off.
4. Pulse your shallots and onions in a food processor or cut them by hand.
5. Leave about 1 to 2 tablespoons of the fat in one of the pans. Add shallot and onion to the pan, and cook over medium heat until they start to caramelize. Add the garlic and cook for about one more minute.
6. Add the chili powder and smoked paprika. Stir to combine.

TIP:
• You can substitute Hormel Black Label Jalapeño Bacon with a black peppered bacon or have your local deli prepare it for you.

"Don't be afraid to tinker. A pimento cheeseburger is a great example of tinkering at its finest—people either love pimento cheese, or they hate it. In my quest to make the best, I discovered that mayo was the one ingredient people disliked. It started me on journey to get rid of mayo and led me to Aunt Martha's suggestion to use ranch dressing. It's something almost everyone loves, and it comes in some many different flavors. Again, the key is the five senses of taste—salty, sweet, spicy, sour, and savory (umami). Use each in moderation so they don't overpower each other. Be subtle."

—Neil Daniell

DIRECTIONS CONTINUED

7. Increase heat to high and carefully add the bourbon and maple syrup. Bring to a boil, stir, and scrape the pan so all the little bacon bits come loose. Continue boiling for about 2 to 3 minutes.

8. Add vinegar and brown sugar and continue to boil for about 3 minutes.

9. Toss the bacon into the pan, reduce heat to low, and simmer for about 10 minutes. The mixture will thicken and look jam-like in the process.

10. Turn off the stove top. Drain any excess fat off the bacon jam by pouring it through a sieve or use cheesecloth to drain it through.

11. Now you have two options: One, you can pop the mixture into a food processor and pulse until it breaks down more. Or you can leave it chunkier. (I prefer the chunkier look).

12. Transfer to jars and store in the fridge.

13. You can heat it up in the microwave whenever you want to top something with the jam.

SPICY PIMENTO CHEESE:

1. In a large bowl, mix the cheeses, cream cheese, onion, jalapeños, and pimentos.

2. Slowly add the dressing to the mixture and combine to an even consistency.

3. Add the garlic paste, cayenne pepper, salt, and pepper.

4. Adjust as necessary to suit taste.

5. Set aside.

FRIED PICKLE CHIPS:

1. Heat oil to approximately 375°F.

2. Place panko breadcrumbs into pie plate.

3. Put chicken fry into a small bowl.

4. Add buttermilk to the chicken fry to make a batter. Whisk until it's smooth.

5. Working in batches, add pickles to the batter and toss to coat. Then dip pickle chips in panko breadcrumbs, making sure to coat all sides.

6. Fry until golden brown.

7. (See note above if you don't have time to make fried dill pickles.)

BURGERS:

1. Preheat pan/grill to 400°F.

2. Season outside of patty to taste using my steak rub or something equivalent.

3. Cook the burger patties to your desired temperature. ServSafe recommends 155°F, which is medium-well.

4. Top each patty with ¼ cup of spicy pimento cheese dip when the patty is approximately 10°F below your desired final temp. Melt cheese.

ASSEMBLY:

1. Bottom bun, toasted

2. Arugula/green lettuce (enough to cover bottom bun)

3. 1–2 slices tomato

4. 3–4 fried pickle chips

5. Burger patty

6. Pimento cheese, melted

7. 2 slices jalapeño bacon

8. Top bun, toasted

(Note: You can lay the bacon on top of the burger in a traditional "X" pattern, or break each strip in half and use 4 small pieces in a weaved, box pattern. For this burger, I prefer the box pattern.)

Sesame Seared Poke Burger

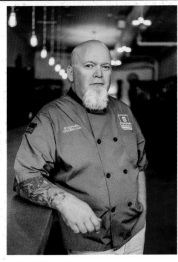

Head Cook:
Stephen Hindman

Team Name:
Stacked, A Montana Grill
Billings, MT

Business Name:
Stacked, A Montana Grill

Facebook:
Stacked, A Montana Grill

www.StackedAMontanaGrill.com

I wanted to create something that was truly surf and turf. I love burgers and I love a great tuna tartar or poke—so many flavors. I make ahi nachos at my restaurant and on a whim, made this recipe. It was a hit and I served it for a while, however, between the cost and the work that goes into making it, decided it was a special night burger only so that I could execute it. Then, going to Alabama (from Montana) meant that I would have direct access to fresh seafood, and so the Ahi Poke Burger was created. Getting to talk to Bo Jackson after the competition and having him and his wife tell me it was the best burger they ever had made all the effort and creativity worthwhile.

Prep Time: 45 Minutes | Cook Time: 15 Minutes | Makes 4–6 servings

Ingredients

TERIYAKI SAUCE:
1 cup pineapple juice
½ cup soy sauce
10 tablespoons brown sugar
2 tablespoons honey
½ cup water
4 tablespoons corn starch

POKE SAUCE:
4 tablespoons soy sauce
1 teaspoon sesame oil
1 teaspoon honey

AHI TUNA:
Ahi tuna steaks (fresh is best; 1 ahi for 2 burgers)
Black and/or white sesame seeds
Poke sauce (recipe below)
Green onion, chopped

WONTON SHREDS:
Cooking oil
Wonton skins (2 per burger)

FRESH PICO DE GALLO:
1 green tomato, diced
½ roasted red pepper, diced
¼ red onion, diced
2 tablespoons pickled ginger, chopped
¼ cup fresh cilantro, chopped
1 tablespoon lime juice
Salt, to taste (sparingly, as the ingredients tend to be salt-rich)

FRESH GUACAMOLE:
2 cups chunky avocado pulp or freshly mashed avocados
1 jalapeño, diced
¼ red onion, diced
¼ cup fresh cilantro, chopped
1 tablespoon lime juice
Salt, to taste (sparingly, as the ingredients tend to be salt-rich)

RED CAVIAR: (In place of Habanero Massago if not available)
Habanero, finely minced
Red caviar

CHANTILLY WASABI CREAM:
2 cups heavy cream
¼ cup chunky avocado spread
1 tablespoon wasabi paste, or to taste

BURGERS:
⅓ pound ground beef per burger (I used Bo's Burgers for the competition, but also recommend an 80/20 ground chuck so you can decide burger thickness. ⅓ lb. is my go-to size)
4–6 sesame buns (find something nice and firm from your local baker that will hold up to all the juiciness of this burger)
¼ cup finely shredded carrots

Directions

TERIYAKI SAUCE:
1. Combine pineapple juice, soy sauce, brown sugar, and honey and bring to simmer.
2. Combine water and corn starch and whisk into sauce, beating and stirring until sauce thickens to desired thickness. (You'll know it's thick enough when it clings nicely to the back of a spoon.)

POKE SAUCE:
1. Combine soy sauce, sesame oil, and honey.
2. Stir briskly with a whisk, until combined, and set aside.

BURGERS:
1. Gently combine ground beef and shredded carrots into ½-pound patties.
2. Season burger with black pepper to taste.
3. Coat patties in teriyaki sauce and pierce burger multiple times with a skewer to allow them to marinate while burgers wait for cooking.

AHI TUNA:
1. Crust top and bottom of ahi steaks with sesame seeds.

"Food, of the people for the people."

—Stephen Hindman

DIRECTIONS CONTINUED

2. Lightly pan sear the ahi steaks in oil to add crust but keeping ahi center rare to medium-rare.

3. Filet the steaks so that you have two sides, both with the rare and seared portions. Cut these into ¼- to ½-inch cubes.

4. Lightly and gently coat with poke sauce.

5. Add desired amount of chopped green onion, mix gently, and set aside to marinate.

WONTON SHREDS:

1. Preheat cooking oil in saucepan (or fryer) to 350°F maximum.

2. While oil is heating, cut wonton wraps into ⅛-inch shreds.

3. Fry shreds in small quantities in oil until crispy and golden.

4. Set aside to drain on paper towel.

FRESH PICO DE GALLO:

1. Combine diced green tomato, diced roasted red pepper, diced onion, chopped ginger, chopped cilantro, dash of lime juice, and dash of salt.

2. Set aside.

FRESH GUACAMOLE:

1. Combine avocado spread, diced jalapeño, diced red onion, chopped cilantro, lime juice, and salt.

2. Set aside.

RED CAVIAR:

1. Mince habanero extra fine and combine with red caviar. Set aside to chill for topping.

CHANTILLY WASABI CREAM:

1. In a blender or mixer, combine 2 cups heavy cream, ¼ cup avocado spread, and wasabi paste to taste. (I think it's better with a little kick with the umami in this burger.)

2. Whip until mixture begins to thicken. You want crème, *not* whipped cream.

BURGERS (CONTINUED):

1. Grill burgers to your preferred doneness, adding additional layers of teriyaki glaze during cooking. This is best done in a cast iron pan to get a nice crust and glaze.

2. Butter buns and grill open-faced in a skillet or on a griddle until golden and crispy.

ASSEMBLY:

1. Bun heel
2. Burger
3. Guacamole
4. Pico
5. Ahi
6. Wonton shreds
7. Chantilly
8. Red caviar
9. Highlight with black caviar
10. Top with bun crown and skewer with a chopstick (or two, and use them for the fun morsels that fall out that you'll be wanting to enjoy)

Head Cook:
Atsuko Ogiya

Team Name:
Shogun Burger
Tokyo, JP

Business Name:
Shogun Burger

Instagram:
@ShogunBurger

www.Shogun-Burger.com

Sukiyaki is an iconic Japanese cuisine, which is the best way to enjoy Wagyu beef, according to Chef Ogiya. This is a "reconstructed" Sukiyaki expressed as a hamburger with some localized flavor profiles by using local products and ingredients. Sukiyaki Burger (as it says "Dallas version") has been one of the most popular brunch items served at their restaurant in Shinjuku ever since they opened. Chef Ogiya felt confident enough to bring it to the competition.

Cook Time: 30 Minutes | Makes 1 serving

Ingredients

SUKIYAKI SAUCE:

½ cup water

½ teaspoon bonito flakes

1 teaspoon soy sauce

1 teaspoon sweet Japanese wine

½ teaspoon brown sugar syrup

1 teaspoon sugar

1 teaspoon ginger paste

1 teaspoon starch

¼ ounce BBQ sauce (I used Sweet Baby Ray's Original Barbecue Sauce)

TARTAR SAUCE:

1 tablespoon mayonnaise

1 teaspoon Japanese mayonnaise (I used Kewpie)

¼ Gherkin cucumber pickle

1 teaspoon Gherkin pickled juice

1 teaspoon salt

⅓ teaspoon onion powder

½ teaspoon brown sugar syrup

FRIED EGG:

¼ ounce lotus root

1 egg

2 dashes Sukiyaki sauce (recipe below)

TEMPURA:

1 cup rice oil

Poultry seasoning, to taste (I used 2 Gringo's Chupacabra Cluckalicious)

Tempura powder

1 ounce crown daisy leaves

⅔ cup water

BURGER:

10 ounces Wagyu beef patty, divided x 2

1 burger bun

1 teaspoon mayonnaise

1 green leaf lettuce

1 onion, sliced (⅛" thick)

1 ounce American white cheddar, divided x 2

¾ ounce Muenster cheese, divided x 2

2 perilla leaves

½ ounce Japanese scallion

2 teaspoons yuzu butter

Black pepper

1 teaspoon unsalted butter

Chili pepper (just to sprinkle)

TIPS:

- You can substitute Wagyu ground beef with ground top ribeye steak or any other ground heavily marbled meat with a high fat content.

- Given the unique nature of this recipe, some ingredients may be hard to find and substitute, depending on where you live.

Directions

PREP:

1. Peel off lotus root, dice, and place in water for 10 minutes.
2. Wash green leaf, scallions, and crown daisies with filtered water.
3. Put smoking wood chips in a pan and fire them up. Put aluminum foil on the chips and line the sliced onions.
4. Put a lid on the pan and leave it for 20 minutes to smoke.
5. Grill scallions with a gas grill until the surface of the leek gets burnt. Cut the leek into 1" pieces and peel off the burnt skins.

SUKIYAKI SAUCE:

1. Put about ½ cup of water and ½ teaspoon of bonito flakes into a pan and heat up.
2. Add soy sauce, Japanese sweet wine, sugar, brown sugar syrup, and ginger paste.
3. Once it boils, add starch to thicken the sauce.
4. Turn off the stove then leave it until it gets cold.
5. Add the BBQ sauce and mix well.

TARTAR SAUCE:

1. Chop and dice cucumber pickles and put into a bowl.
2. Add mayonnaise, Kewpie mayonnaise, pickled juice, onion powder, brown sugar syrup, and salt. Mix well.

FRIED EGG:

1. Preheat the griddle to 390°F.
2. Put diced lotus root into a circle on the griddle and crack an egg into it.
3. Crash the egg yolk and mix it roughly.
4. Add 2 dashes of the Sukiyaki sauce.

PATTY:

1. Make sure the griddle is still 390°F.
2. Lightly form 2 5-oz ground beef balls, then put them on the griddle.
3. Smash the meat with a smasher and keep pressing for 5 seconds.
4. Take off the smasher and sprinkle with poultry seasoning. Cook for 4 minutes.
5. Flip the patty and sprinkle the seasoning.
6. Put two kinds of cheese on top of the patty.
7. Put on a basting cover then leave it for 3–5 minutes, depending on the condition of the griddle.

> *"To create a dish, the most important thing is inspiration. To be inspired, the most important thing is to imagine customers' smiles when they eat their dish."*
>
> —Atsuko Ogiya

DIRECTIONS CONTINUED

8. Open the cover then sprinkle black pepper over the patty.

9. Optional: To make it a double cheeseburger, repeat the above process one more time.

TEMPURA:

1. Preheat rice oil in a pan at 355°F.

2. Prepare a bowl of cold water. Add tempura powder and seasoning. Mix roughly.

3. Cut a crown daisy to 6" with 3–4 branches.

4. Put the crown daisy into the tempura batter.

5. Deep fry the crown daisy with the rice oil until it gets crispy and a nice golden color.

BUNS:

1. Prewarm unsalted butter.

2. Brush the butter oil on the inside surface of both burger buns.

3. Slightly toast the buns only on the side with butter oil.

ASSEMBLY:

1. Spread the mayonnaise on the heel bun.

2. Spread yuzu butter on the crown bun.

3. Heel bun

4. Green leaf

5. Smoked onion

6. Beef patty

7. Melted cheese (2 kinds)

8. Sukiyaki sauce

9. Perilla leaf

10. Beef patty

11. Melted cheese (2 kinds)

12. Sukiyaki sauce

13. Lotus root fried egg

14. Perilla leaf

15. Japanese scallion

16. Chili pepper

17. Crown daisy tempura

18. Tartar sauce

19. Crown bun

20. Put a skewer through the center of the burger

Spicy Gangnam-Style Veggie Burger

The challenge for this round of competition was to use sponsor products and create unique flavor profiles and techniques for a plant-based vegetarian burger. My concept features some of my favorite flavor combinations. I used American Saison ale four ways in this Korean fusion veggie burger, first using the ale to make a shandy syrup with Asian spices and flavors added, and some used as a dressing for the red cabbage and danmuji (pickled daikon radish) slaw, and the rest thickened and used as a glaze for the burger patties. The ale was also used in the Ssamjang, mushroom BBQ jam, and beer-battered whiskey cornichon fries.

The reason I chose to compete with this type of flavor profile was because the combination of spicy, sweet, sour and umami-packed flavors hit all the right notes that we love to experience when we eat! My favorite element in this dish was using the ale in unique ways in the various components of this burger, each one complementing the other in one delicious bite after another!

Cook Time: 50 Minutes | Makes 6 servings

Head Cook:
Sandi Sheppard

Team Name:
Sandi Sheppard
Norman, OK

Facebook:
@Sandi.Sheppard1

Instagram:
@SandiShep7

Twitter:
@SandiSheppard

TIPS:
- Criminis are a different name for baby portobello mushrooms.
- You can substitute an Asian pear with a bartlett or bosc pear.

Ingredients

SHANDY SYRUP (BURGER GLAZE & SLAW DRESSING):

16 ounces beer (I used Boulevard Beer Tank 7)

1 cup brown sugar

½ cup thawed lemonade concentrate

2 teaspoons granulated sweetener (I used Pyure Organic Granulated Sweetener)

¼ cup soy sauce

¼ cup seasoned rice vinegar

1 tablespoon ginger paste

1 teaspoon sesame oil

½ teaspoon cayenne pepper (I used Fiesta)

½ teaspoon chili lime seasoning blend (I used Fiesta)

¼ teaspoon garlic, chopped in oil (I used Fiesta)

¼ teaspoon kosher salt

2 tablespoons cornstarch with 2 tablespoons water

BEER SSAMJANG MUSHROOM BBQ JAM:

1 tablespoon grapeseed oil

8 ounces crimini mushrooms, coarsely chopped in blender

1 cup sweet yellow onion, diced

1 red bell pepper, chopped

½ tablespoon garlic, chopped in oil (I used Fiesta)

¾ cup beer (I used Boulevard Tank 7 American Saison Ale)

6 ounces tomato paste (I used Red Gold Tomato Paste)

3 tablespoons Ssamjang

2 tablespoons BBQ sauce (I used John Boy & Billy's Sweet & Mild BBQ Sauce)

14.5 ounce can petite diced tomatoes (I used Red Gold Petite Diced Tomatoes)

1 tablespoon sweet soy glaze

1 tablespoon black truffle hot sauce

1 tablespoon vegetable base

½ tablespoon porcini mushroom seasoning blend

1 teaspoon liquid smoke

½ teaspoon cayenne pepper (I used Fiesta)

½ teaspoon kosher salt

¼ teaspoon ground white pepper (I used Fiesta)

¼ teaspoon ground nutmeg (I used Fiesta)

¼ teaspoon ground cardamom (I used Fiesta)

RED CABBAGE & DANMUJI SLAW:

2 cups shredded red cabbage

1 Asian pear, peeled, cored, and cubed

1 cup shredded carrot

2 scallions, chopped (both white and green parts)

1 cup pickled daikon radish, cubed (danmuji)

SPICY TRUFFLE MUSTARD & PORCINI AIOLI:

1–½ cups vegan mayonnaise

3 ounces cream cheese

½ tablespoon garlic, chopped in oil (I used Fiesta)

2 tablespoons truffle mustard

1 teaspoon porcini mushroom seasoning

½ teaspoon wasabi paste

¼ teaspoon kosher salt

¼ teaspoon ground white pepper (I used Fiesta)

2 tablespoons pepper blend (I used Rozie's Extra Hot RelSa)

BEER-BATTERED WHISKEY CORNICHON FRIES:

2 cups oil

¾ cup beer (I used Boulevard Tank 7 American Saison Ale)

½ cup self-rising flour

1 tablespoon cornstarch

¼ teaspoon ground cardamom (I used Fiesta)

¼ teaspoon cayenne pepper (I used Fiesta)

¼ teaspoon ground nutmeg (I used Fiesta)

¼ teaspoon ground white pepper (I used Fiesta)

¼ teaspoon kosher salt

2 12.5-ounce jars whiskey cornichon pickles

SPICY GANGNAM STYLE VEGGIE BURGERS:

2¼ pounds plant-based meat (I used Impossible Burger)

1 tablespoon hickory liquid smoke

½ tablespoon chili lime seasoning blend (I used Fiesta)

2 teaspoons ground cardamom (I used Fiesta)

2 teaspoons cayenne pepper (I used Fiesta)

1 tablespoon kosher salt

½ tablespoon ground black pepper (I used Fiesta)

CIABATTA BUNS:

6 ciabatta buns

Olive oil cooking spray

¼ cup butter, melted

2 tablespoons porcini seasoning blend

2 tablespoons sesame seeds

MISCELLANEOUS INGREDIENTS:

¼ cup butter, melted

1–2 tablespoons porcini mushroom seasoning

Vegetable oil for frying

Mild chili threads

Green leaves of choice

Directions

SHANDY SYRUP (BURGER GLAZE & SLAW DRESSING):

1. Place beer in a saucepan on medium-low.

2. Whisk in the brown sugar, sweetener, and lemonade and simmer for 10 minutes.

3. Whisk in soy sauce, rice vinegar, ginger paste, sesame oil, cayenne pepper, chili lime seasoning, chopped garlic, and salt. Continue simmering for 15 more minutes.

4. Pour ¾ cup of mixture into a small container and set aside for the slaw.

5. Dissolve cornstarch in water, stirring, and whisk into the remaining mixture in saucepan. Continue simmering for another 5 minutes, then remove from heat. Cover.

BEER SSAMJUNG MUSHROOM BBQ JAM:

1. Sauté the mushrooms and bell pepper with the onion for 3 minutes.

2. Add remaining ingredients and simmer until thickened.

3. Cover and set aside.

RED CABBAGE & DANMUJI SLAW:

1. Add all ingredients into a gallon-sized resealable bag and stir in the reserved shandy syrup.

2. Seal, forcing the air out of the bag, and lay flat so that the liquid coats all of the ingredients.

SPICY TRUFFLE MUSTARD & PORCINI AIOLI:

1. Mix the ingredients into small bowl and chill until needed.

BEER-BATTERED WHISKEY CORNICHON FRIES:

1. Heat vegetable oil on medium heat.

2. Mix the beer with the flour, cornstarch, spices, and salt.

3. Cut the pickles in half lengthwise and dry with paper towels.

4. Use tongs to dip pickle pieces into the flour mixture. Let excess batter drip off and fry in 2 batches in oil until nicely browned.

5. Put onto a wire rack over a baking sheet and into a warm oven (200°F).

SPICY GANGNAM STYLE VEGGIE BURGERS:

1. Mix ingredients and form into 6 patties of equal size.

2. Frying in batches, place onto a preheated and oil-sprayed cast iron plancha and cook 3 minutes.

3. Salt and pepper the tops, then turn and brush patties with shandy glaze and cook another 3 minutes.

4. Place onto a baking sheet and into a 200°F oven until ready to assemble.

CIABATTA BUNS:

1. Spray cut sides with olive oil spray and broil until nicely browned.

2. Remove, turn oven up to 350°F, brush top buns with butter, dust with porcini seasoning and sesame seeds, and heat for 5 minutes.

3. Top buns with chili threads.

ASSEMBLY:

1. Coat the cut side of buns with aioli.

2. Place a green leaf on all bottom buns and top with a glazed burger patty.

3. Add a generous amount of the mushroom jam, topped with drained slaw.

4. Finish with cornichon fries on each and close with the top bun.

5. Skewer a scallion onto the top and sprinkle with chili threads.

6. Serve and enjoy!

I like to call this recipe "The Whole Enchilada," for it has all the flavors of an enchilada, one of my favorites, all wrapped up. I love the surprise of the injected avocado within the burger and the crispy cactus-shaped tortilla chip as a cute little side treat. I wanted to push the envelope with this recipe and using a tortilla to envelop the burger was certainly different.

Cook Time: 48 Minutes | Makes 6 servings

Head Cook:
Susanne Duplantis

Team Name:
Makeover My Leftover
New Roads, LA

Business Name:
Makeover My Leftover

Facebook:
Makeover My Leftover

Instagram:
www.MakeoverMyLeftover.com

Ingredients

HOMEMADE CHILI POWDER:
1 medium dried Ancho chile
½ teaspoon cumin seed, toasted
½ teaspoon dried Mexican oregano
¼ teaspoon garlic powder

TOMATILLO SALSA:
2 tomatillos, husked, rinsed, halved
1 poblano pepper
2 Roma tomatoes, halved
1 small purple onion, diced
2 ounces chunky avocado spread (I used Walmart Brand)
Salt, to taste

CACTUS TORTILLA CHIPS:
2 10-inch flour tortillas
Olive oil

ENCHILADA SAUCE:
¼ teaspoon olive oil
1 tablespoon taco seasoning
¼ teaspoon cayenne
¼ teaspoon paprika
Homemade chili powder (see recipe)
10 ounces Mexican beer
8 ounces tomato sauce (I used Red Gold Tomato Sauce)
1 tablespoon unsalted butter (I used Challenge Unsalted Butter)
1 tablespoon flour

BURGERS:
2 pounds ground angus beef (I used 1 bag Bo's Grand Slam Burgers)
¼ pound beef chorizo

½ pound ground ribeye
1 garlic clove, minced
1 tablespoon red chili adobe
1 tablespoon taco seasoning
1 tablespoon olive oil
1 onion, sliced
1 red bell pepper, sliced
1 yellow bell pepper, sliced
1 green bell pepper, sliced
1 orange bell pepper, sliced
1 cup Mexican rice, cooked
2 cups quesadilla cheese
6 10-inch flour tortillas
6 ounces chunky avocado spread (I used Walmart Brand)
Juice of 1 lime
2 ounces Mexican beer

Directions

HOMEMADE CHILI POWDER:
1. Dampen dried Ancho chili and toast for 4 minutes in 350°F oven.
2. Remove seeds and steam, then tear into pieces. Add to mini food processor. Pulse with cumin seeds, oregano, and garlic powder until fine. Set aside.

TOMATILLO SALSA
1. Rub tomatillos, poblano, and tomatoes with olive oil. Bake for 15 minutes at 350°F. Remove pepper skin. Add to processor with dash of salt. Pulse for salsa. Mix with 2 ounces chunky avocado and purple onion.

CACTUS TORTILLA CHIPS:
1. Using cookie cutters, cut out cactus shapes out of tortillas, and put on sheet pan. Brush with olive oil and bake 7 minutes at 350°F.

ENCHILADA SAUCE:
1. In a skillet over medium heat with ¼ teaspoon olive oil, toast 1 tablespoon taco seasoning, paprika, and cayenne over low heat, about 1 minute until it resembles coffee grinds.
2. Stir in homemade chili powder.
3. Raise heat to medium. Add tomato sauce and can of beer. Simmer for 10 minutes.
4. Using hands, knead butter and flour together until well incorporated for

a beurre manié (equal parts softened butter and flour blended together to help thicken sauces). Raise heat and bring to a boil. Whisk in beurre manié for 1 minute. Remove from heat.

BURGERS:
1. Using hands, mix burger meat with chorizo, ribeye, garlic, red chili adobe, and 1 tablespoon taco seasoning. Form into patties.
2. Heat a cast iron skillet over medium-high heat with olive oil. Add burgers and cook 4½ minutes. Flip, brush with enchilada sauce, and cook 3 minutes. Remove.
3. Add peppers and onions to skillet and sauté for 5 minutes.

"My motto is 'To cook is to create.' I like to think outside the icebox and competing certainly releases the best inner culinary artist in us all."

—Susanne Duplantis

DIRECTIONS CONTINUED

4. Lay out tortillas. Top each tortilla center with rice, sautéed onions, peppers, and cheese.

5. Place burger on top of mixture.

6. Fold tortilla around burger.

7. Place tortilla seam side down in skillet over medium heat.

8. Cook 1 minute.

9. Flip. Cook an additional 30 seconds. Remove.

10. In a small bowl, mix 1 teaspoon lime juice and beer into remaining chunky avocado spread.

11. Using an injector, inject quesadillas with avocado mixture.

12. Serve with tomatillo salsa and cactus tortilla chip.

A marinated and seasoned Impossible burger served over crispy green lettuce, topped with a Boulevard Brewing Tank 7 Saison ale, garlic chili cheddar beer cheese sauce, Tank 7 beer-battered onion straws, a made-from-scratch Tank 7-based BBQ sauce, and chopped green onions on a freshly baked Tank 7 infused hamburger bun! The inspiration behind this was to incorporate Tank 7 into every element of the burger since it was the required infused ingredient that we had to use in that year's Top 10 round.

Head Cook:
Tommy Shive

Team Name:
Tommy Shive
Memphis, TN

Facebook:
Tommy Shive

Prep Time: 30 Minutes | Cook Time: 20 Minutes | Makes 6 servings

Ingredients

BEER BUNS: (YIELDS 6 BUNS)

2 tablespoons fast rise yeast

¾ cup warm beer (I used Boulevard Brewing Tank 7)

3–3½ cups bread flour

¼ cup warm water

⅓ cup vegetable oil

¼ cup sugar

1 large egg, beaten

1 teaspoon salt

CRISPY BEER BATTERED ONION STRAWS:

2 pounds onion

6 tablespoons all-purpose flour

1 cup beer (I used Boulevard Brewing Tank 7)

4 cups buttermilk

GARLIC CHILI CHEDDAR BEER CHEESE:

6 tablespoons unsalted butter

1 cup beer (I used Boulevard Brewing Tank 7)

2 cups heavy cream

1½ teaspoon vegan Worcestershire sauce

1 teaspoon kosher salt

1 teaspoon granulated garlic

1 teaspoon black pepper

½ teaspoon cayenne pepper

6 cups shredded garlic chili cheddar cheese

BURGERS:

Plant-based burger patties (I used Impossible Burgers)

½ cup hot sauce (I used Cholula)

½ cup vegan Worcestershire sauce

½ cup beer (I used Boulevard Brewing Tank 7)

All-purpose seasoning, to taste (I used Boars Night Out White Lighting)

BBQ seasoning, to taste (I used JRG Rusty Dust, or use your favorite BBQ seasoning)

BBQ sauce

Green onion, chopped

Lettuce

BBQ BEER SAUCE:

1¼ cups ketchup

1 cup turbinado raw cane sugar

¼ cup molasses

¼ cup pineapple juice

¼ cup beer (I used Boulevard Brewing Tank 7 beer)

1 tablespoon vegan Worcestershire sauce

2½ teaspoons ground mustard

2 teaspoons smoked paprika

½ teaspoon garlic powder

¼ teaspoon cayenne powder

1½ kosher salt

1 teaspoon pepper

2–3 tablespoons BBQ rub of choice (I used JRG Rusty Dust)

1 tablespoon Dijon mustard

1 tablespoon + ½ teaspoon dry mustard

Directions

BEER BUNS:

1. Preheat oven to 400°F.
2. Warm beer and water to 95–105°F, then add yeast and dissolve.
3. Add oil and sugar, then let sit for 5 minutes.
4. Add beaten eggs, salt, and flour, and mix well.
5. Turn onto floured surface and knead for 3–5 minutes. Immediately divide and shape into balls and place on a mat (ex. Silpat) and let rest for 20 minutes.
6. Bake for 10–12 minutes.

BURGERS:

1. Measure out 5 ounces of plant-based meat and form into balls.
2. Use burger press to press all into patties.
3. In a small missing bowl, combine vegan Worcestershire sauce, hot sauce, and beer and stir.
4. Using a pastry brush, gently brush mixture on both sides of formed burger patties.
5. Place patties on cookie sheet and chill until ready to grill.

CRISPY BEER-BATTERED ONION STRAWS:

1. Heat oil in pot to 350°F.
2. Thinly slice onions and soak in buttermilk.
3. Combine flour with beer to form a batter.
4. Remove onions from buttermilk and shake off excess milk.
5. Dip in batter and fry until crispy.

"If more of us valued food and cheer and song above hoarded gold, it would be a merrier world."

—J.R.R. Tolkien

DIRECTIONS CONTINUED

6. Place a cookie sheet lined with paper towels. Sprinkle with salt.

BBQ BEER SAUCE:

1. Combine all ingredients into a saucepan and whisk together until smooth.

2. Bring to a boil over medium-high heat.

3. After it starts bubbling, reduce the heat to a simmer and cook for an additional 6–7 minutes.

GARLIC CHILI CHEDDAR BEER CHEESE:

1. In a large pot, heat butter until melted and add flour to form a roux.

2. Add beer while whisking to keep lumps from forming.

3. Slowly add in heavy cream while whisking and cook until mixture thickens.

4. After mixture is thickened, add Worcestershire sauce, salt, pepper, garlic powder, cayenne, and stir.

5. Add in shredded cheese half cup at a time and stir until completely melted.

BURGERS (CONTINUED):

1. Heat grill or flattop to 350°F.

2. Remove burgers from fridge. Lightly season both side of patties with all-purpose and BBQ seasonings.

3. Place on grill and cook on 4–5 minutes on each side, or until internal temp is 160°F.

4. Cut buns in half and gently brush with melted butter and lightly toast.

5. After buns are toasted, place bottom bun on plate and top with crispy green lettuce, followed by a burger patty.

6. Gently pour beer cheese sauce in middle until it spreads to edge of burger.

7. Top the beer cheese with beer-battered onion straws, followed by a drizzle of BBQ sauce.

8. Garnish with chopped green onion, skewer top bun, and place on top of onion straws.

9. Enjoy!

Head Cook:
Dan Hodgins

Team Name:
Chicken Chokers BBQ
Fair Lawn, NJ

Facebook:
Chicken Chokers BBQ

www.ChickenChokersBar-B-Que.com

A juicy wagyu hamburger rubbed with Chupacabra Brisket Magic, stuffed with pimento cheese, topped with a housemade chipotle burger sauce, Havarti cheese, baked onion, a red and green roasted hatch chili relish with a bacon chipotle BBQ sauce served on a brioche bun.

Cook Time: 1 Hour, 15 Minutes | Makes 6 servings

Ingredients

TEXAS TWINKIES:

12 ounces Wagyu ground beef

1 shallot, diced

½ tablespoon beef brine (I used DB180 Beef Brine)

½ tablespoon meat seasoning (I used Chupacabra Brisket Magic Rub)

½ tablespoon meat seasoning (I used Chupacabra Special Blend)

½ tablespoon meat seasoning (I used Backyard Better Burger Blend)

½ tablespoon butter

4 ounces cheddar cheese, shredded

8 ounces pimento cheese

8 ounces cream cheese

1 tablespoon cheesy seasoning (I used PS Grate State Cheesy Blend)

6 jalapeños, hollowed out with seeds removed

6 slices bacon

¼ cup bacon chipotle BBQ sauce, for glaze at the end (recipe below)

RELISH:

1 cup chili relish, drained (I used Fresh Chile Company Hatch Red & Green Chili Relish)

½ tablespoon seasoning (I used Chupacabra Seasoning)

½ tablespoon citrus seasoning (I used Feiny's Citrus Dust Rub)

½ tablespoon honey (I used North Texas Honey Mesquite, Cotton, Tallow Tree & Wildflower Honey)

1 teaspoon bacon chipotle BBQ sauce, drained (I used Bob's Foods Smoked Bacon Chipotle BBQ Sauce)

BACON CHIPOTLE BBQ SAUCE:

1½ cups bacon chipotle BBQ sauce, drained (I used Bob's Foods Smoked Bacon Chipotle BBQ Sauce)

1 tablespoon brisket seasoning (I used Chupacabra Brisket Magic)

1 tablespoon chili relish, drained (I used Fresh Chile Company Hatch Red & Green Chili Relish)

½ tablespoon honey (I used Runamok Honey)

1 tablespoon Wagyu bacon chipotle jelly (I used Hassell Brand)

HOMEMADE CHIPOTLE BURGER SAUCE:

3 ounces chipotle ketchup

2 ounces regular ketchup

3 ounces light mayonnaise

2 ounces bacon aioli squeeze (I used Terrapin Ridge Farms)

½ teaspoon citrus seasoning (I used Feiny's Citrus Rub)

½ teaspoon meat seasoning (I used Chupacabra Special Blend Seasoning)

GRILLED ONION RINGS:

2 yellow onions, sliced into ¼-inch slices

2 tablespoons seasoning (I used Chupacabra Chop House Blend)

Cooking spray with oil

BACON:

1 pound bacon

All-purpose seasoning, to taste (I used Chupacabra Ribnoxious Blend)

BURGERS:

48 ounces Wagyu beef (I used Hassell Cattle Company Wagyu Beef)

2½ tablespoons burger seasoning (I used Backyard Better Burger Rub)

2½ tablespoons all-purpose seasoning (I used Chupacabra Chop House Blend)

2½ tablespoons brisket seasoning (I used Chupacabra Brisket Magic)

2 tablespoons beef brine (I used DB180 Beef Brine)

2 tablespoons bacon chipotle BBQ sauce

1 ounce BBQ sauce (I used John Boy & Billy's Grilling Sauce)

9 tablespoons pimento cheese (I used Queen Charlotte's Pimento Cheese Royal)

1 slice Havarti cheese, per burger

6 toasted brioche buns

ASSEMBLY:

1 head romaine lettuce

Candied jalapeños (I used Old Montgomery Candied Jalapeños)

Directions

TEXAS TWINKIES:

1. Sauté ground beef and shallots with beef brine and meat seasonings in butter. Drain and let cool.

2. Mix cheeses and add rubs and cooled ground beef. Mix well.

3. Hollow out jalapeños and remove the seeds.

4. Stuff jalapeños with cheese and meat mixture.

5. Wrap each jalapeño with bacon.

6. Dust with meat seasoning.

7. Put in 350°F oven until done, about 25 minutes.

8. Towards the end, brush with bacon chipotle BBQ sauce (recipe below) to glaze and caramelize.

RELISH:

1. Combine all seasonings, honey, and BBQ sauce and thicken in a saucepan.

2. Add drained chili relish.

BACON CHIPOTLE BBQ SAUCE:

1. Combine the first four ingredients and simmer to thicken.

2. Once slightly cooled, stir in Wagyu bacon jelly.

HOMEMADE CHIPOTLE BURGER SAUCE:

1. Combine all ingredients together and stir.

GRILLED ONION RINGS:

1. Place onion rings on a cookie sheet, spray with oil, and sprinkle with seasoning on both sides.

2. Bake in oven at 350°F until soft and golden in color.

BACON:

1. Place bacon on a rack/cookie sheet and sprinkle both sides with poultry seasoning.

2. Bake in oven at 350°F for 20 minutes, or until crispy.

BURGERS:

1. Divide the meat into 4-ounce patties. Place 1½ tablespoons pimento cheese on top of one patty. Place second patty on top and form burger. Sprinkle with beef brine.

2. Combine all 3 seasonings into shaker. Sprinkle on top of each burger.

3. Grill burger to desired doneness.

4. Glaze with the bacon chipotle BBQ sauce.

5. Melt cheese on top.

6. Toast brioche bun.

ASSEMBLY:

1. Spread both sides of toasted bun with homemade burger sauce. On bottom bun, place romaine lettuce.

2. Place grilled burger with melted cheese on top of lettuce.

3. Top with 2 onion rings.

4. Fill the center of the onion rings with chili relish.

5. Top with bacon slices and place top bun on burger.

6. Skewer Texas Twinkie and place on top of burger.

7. Garnish with candied jalapeños.

Head Cook:
Doug Keiles

Team Name:
Ribs Within
Gloucester, MA

Facebook:
Doug Keiles

Instagram: @
MeatAndSweetFoods

www.RibsWithin.com

A BBQ-seasoned bacon onion burger topped with handcrafted uncured applewood bacon jam, bacon fat-braised onions, melted Muenster cheese, and an avocado jalapeño bacon jam special sauce, all on a perfectly toasted onion pocket bun.

Cook Time: 30 Minutes | Makes 4–6 servings

Ingredients

APPLEWOOD BACON JAM:

2 pounds uncured applewood smoked bacon, chopped

2 tablespoons bacon fat

Canola cooking spray

1 cup onion, chopped

1 tablespoon Texas BBQ rub

2 tablespoons beef rub (I used Wahoo Beef BBQ Rub)

1 tablespoon balsamic vinegar

1 tablespoon brown sugar

1 small jalapeño, diced

1 tablespoon BBQ sauce (I used John Boy & Billy's Grillin' Sauce)

BURGERS:

Hamburger meat $70/30$ or $75/25$ or Blended Bo Jackson Burger

Beef rub, to season

Texas rub, to season

6 slices Muenster cheese

6 slices bacon

3 large onions, sliced and halved

AVOCADO BURGER SAUCE:

¼ cup mayonnaise

2 halves jalapeños, finely chopped

1 tablespoon bacon jam (recipe below)

1 package chunky avocado spread

Directions

APPLEWOOD BACON JAM:

1. Over medium high heat, cook chopped bacon until almost crispy.
2. Drain fat and reserve.
3. Heat a nonstick sauté pan with canola spray and 1 tablespoon bacon fat on medium high.
4. When hot, add 1 more tablespoon of bacon fat and add onions.
5. Sauté onions until soft and tan, then add BBQ and beef rub. Set aside.
6. Add cooked onions to the cooked bacon for jam, balsamic vinegar, beef rub, brown sugar, and diced jalapeño and add to mix.
7. Add BBQ sauce.
8. Blend until almost smooth and set aside.

BURGERS:

1. On a disposable cutting board, combine beef.
2. Spread meat into a thin layer (¼").
3. Shake beef rub heavily over entire area.

4. Shake Texas rub lightly over entire area.
5. Use your fingertips to push rub down into meat.
6. Make into meatballs.
7. Flatten each meatball down to 1" patties.
8. Sprinkle beef rub on both sides of each patty.
9. Press down on the middle of each burger to form a slight indent.
10. Grill burgers until 120°F.
11. Remove from grill and put into disposable half pan.
12. Top each burger with 2 ounces of bacon jam and 2 ounces of sautéed onions.
13. Place a slice of Muenster cheese on each burger.
14. Put back on grill on medium heat for 3 minutes or until 142–145° and the cheese is melted.
15. Remove from grill and cover with aluminum foil after 3–4 minutes.

AVOCADO BURGER SAUCE:

1. Combine mayonnaise, chopped jalapeños, bacon jam, and chunky avocado spread.
2. Mix all ingredients and keep cold until use.

BUNS:

1. Brush both sides of cut bun lightly with bacon fat.
2. On medium, grill both sides of each bun half for 1 minute for crust side, 2 minutes for oiled flat side.

ASSEMBLY:

1. Slather special sauce on both top and bottom buns.
2. Place a burger on a bun bottom.
3. Place top of bun on top of the burger and eat it!

"*Let food be thy medicine and medicine be thy food.*"

—Hippocrates

The Bo Bear Bacon Cheeseburger

Head Cook:
Wade Fortin

Team Name:
Team BULL
Sacramento, CA

Facebook:
Second City Smoke

Instagram:
@WadeRino

TIP:
- You can substitute Wagyu beef bacon with regular bacon.

A Bo Jackson Angus Grand Slam Burger with roasted garlic cheddar, fried pickled honey sweet onions, caramelized onion aioli, marinated beefsteak tomato, spicy ketchup, and candied bacon on a brioche bun.

Cook Time: 1 Hour | Makes 1 serving

Ingredients

1 large onion (I used Little Bear Honey Sweet Onion)

1 burger patty (I used Bo Jackson's Angus Grand Slam Burger)

1 brioche bun

3 tablespoons + ½ teaspoon agave nectar

2 teaspoons buttermilk

1 teaspoon dry onion soup mix

1 tablespoon ketchup

3 dashes tabasco

2 strips bacon

½ teaspoon cracked black pepper

1 tablespoon mayonnaise

1 slice roasted garlic cheese

2 strips Wagyu beef bacon

1 slice beefsteak tomato

1 tablespoon white balsamic vinegar

1 teaspoon olive oil

1 tablespoon steak seasoning

3 tablespoons butter

1 cup flour

½ cup corn starch

4 cups peanut oil for frying

1 cup cider vinegar

Directions

1. Preheat grill on high and pre-heat oven to 375°F.

2. Dice half an onion. Julienne cut the other half and set aside.

3. In a skillet heated on medium-high, add 2 tablespoons of peanut oil. Sauté diced onions until fond forms on bottom of pan.

4. Deglaze with water and repeat until onions turn brown.

5. Add ½ teaspoon agave, mix, and set aside to cool.

6. Mix mayonnaise, buttermilk, 2 teaspoons of caramelized onions, and dry onion soup mix. Set aside.

7. Season bacon with cracked black pepper and cook in oven until almost done. Glaze with 1 tablespoon agave and finish until bacon is candied.

8. Mix ketchup and tabasco set aside.

9. Marinate tomato in white balsamic and olive oil. Season with steak rub.

10. On the stove top, bring cider vinegar and 1 tablespoon of agave to a boil. Remove from heat and add ½ an onion that has been julienned. Set aside to cool.

11. Heat peanut oil to 375°F in a cast iron pot. Mix flour, corn starch, and 1 tablespoon steak seasoning.

12. Once onions have cooled, drain liquid, pat dry, and toss in seasoned flour. Fry and season to taste with steak seasoning.

13. Place beef bacon on sheet pan and bake for 15 minutes or until crispy. Drain fat into a foil half pan.

14. Add butter to pan and place on grill. Season burger patty and place in pan. Cook for 10 minutes on low heat and flip. Cook for another 5 minutes and remove.

15. Place burger on grill turned to low heat, top with minced crispy beef bacon mixed with 1 teaspoon of caramelized onion. Top with one slice of cheese and melt.

16. Toast buns.

17. Place candied bacon on bottom bun, top with 1 slice marinated tomato, burger patty, fried onions, and drizzle with ketchup. Spread aioli on top bun and place on burger.

"First we eat, then we do everything else."

—M.F.K. Fisher

Head Cook:
Damon Holter

Team Name:
Croix Valley
Hudson, WI

Business Name:
Croix Valley Foods

Facebook:
Croix Valley

Instagram:
@CroixValley

www.CroixValleyFoods.com

Inspired by South-of-the-border flavors, the Cantina Burger features a Mexican-spiced ground beef patty set atop chunky guacamole and iceberg lettuce, topped with Spanish-influenced peppers and onions, melted cheeses, and chipotle sour cream! I really enjoy the depth of flavor in using chorizo sausage as a seasoning, and the flavors and texture meld to create the perfect bite.

Cook Time: 25 Minutes | Makes 4–6 servings

Ingredients

BURGERS:

1½ pounds 80% lean ground beef

½ pound ground chuck

2 teaspoons garlic seasoning (I used Croix Valley Garlic Barbecue Booster)

6 ciabatta buns

Garlic butter (see sidebar for recipe)

18 ounces Monterey Jack cheese, shredded

2 cups iceberg lettuce, shredded

4 flour tortillas, cut into ¼" to ½" strips

Canola oil (for frying)

½ cup Mexican seasoning

½ cup sour cream

2 tablespoons chipotle in adobo sauce

½ pound ground chorizo sausage

1 red and 1 orange bell peppers, julienne cut

1 large yellow onion, julienne cut

4-INGREDIENT GUACAMOLE:

1 medium yellow onion, minced

2 cloves garlic, minced

¾ cup diced Roma tomatoes (about 2 tomatoes)

3 avocados, diced

Directions

1. Blend garlic seasoning into ground beef and ground chuck. Form into 6 equal patties (approximately ¼ pound). Season exterior of the patties with approximately ¼ cup (more or less to taste) Mexican spices and grill burger to desired doneness.

2. Spread the garlic butter on the cut insides of the ciabatta buns. Grill on a flat top grill or pan until golden brown.

3. Mix chipotle with adobo into sour cream, set aside.

4. Mix all ingredients together for guacamole, combine, and set aside.

5. Heat 2 tablespoons canola oil and add onions, peppers, and chorizo sausage. Cook over medium-high heat until onions become slightly translucent and peppers have softened to desired doneness. Remove chorizo (save for another use or discard), drain any excess liquid.

6. In small pot, heat 4 cups canola oil to 375°F for frying. Fry tortilla strips until golden brown. Remove from oil, drain on paper towel, and season with remaining Mexican seasoning.

ASSEMBLY:

1. Bottom bun
2. Guacamole
3. Shredded lettuce
4. Burger patty
5. Pepper and onion mix
6. Shredded cheese, melted
7. Fried tortilla strips
8. Chipotle sour cream
9. Top bun

Garlic Butter Recipe

Combine 1 stick softened butter, 2 tablespoons minced garlic, and 1 tablespoon garlic seasoning (I used Croix Valley Garlic Barbecue Booster). Mix thoroughly and set aside for toasting buns.

"Competitive cooking is a melting pot of passion, skill, and creativity, where flavors become the canvas and the elevated food becomes the masterpiece."

—Damon Holter

The Hometown Smashburger

Head Cook:
Morgan Cheek

Team Name:
Sweet Cheeks Pit BBQ
Muscle Shoals, AL

Facebook:
Sweet Cheeks Pit BBQ

Instagram:
@SweetCheeksPitBBQ

These burgers boast two ultra-juicy all beef burger patties, receiving a healthy dusting with our all-American seasoning and a high heat sear on the grill for the most amazing crunchy crust. Topped with melty American cheese, caramelized onions, pickle chips, and brown sugar bourbon bacon on a buttery toasted brioche bun, these burgers will transport you back to your hometown drive-in days.

Cook Time: 1 Hour, 30 Minutes | Makes 11 servings

Ingredients

22 4-ounce burger patties (I used Bo Jackson Grand Slam Burgers)

4 tablespoons salt

4 tablespoons fresh ground black pepper

4 tablespoons onion powder

4 tablespoons garlic powder

4 tablespoons steak seasoning (I used Dale's Steak Seasoning)

6 large honey sweet onions, thinly sliced

8 tablespoons salted butter, divided

11 slices hickory smoked bacon (I used Wright Brand Hickory Smoked Bacon)

1 cup brown sugar bourbon

1¼ cup dark brown sugar

22 slices American cheese

8 tablespoons ketchup

4 tablespoons yellow mustard

8 tablespoons mayonnaise

4 tablespoons BBQ sauce (I used John Boy & Billy's Grillin' Sauce)

4 tablespoons Bloody Mary mix (I used Zing Zang Bloody Mary Mix)

22 pickle ovals chips

11 brioche buns, buttered and toasted

Directions

1. Preheat oven to 400°F.

2. Preheat griddle to 475°F.

3. Combine salt, pepper, garlic powder, and onion powder well for burger seasoning.

4. Place sliced onions in cast iron skillet on stove top on medium heat. After onions have cooked for 10 minutes, add a dash of salt and pepper and 4 tablespoons of butter. Reduce heat to medium-low and continue to cook onions, stirring every few minutes until caramelized, about 15–20 minutes.

5. Mix brown sugar bourbon and dark brown sugar into small saucepan over medium-high heat. Stir to combine. Bring to a boil then reduce to a simmer for 10 minutes. Remove from heat and set aside.

6. Place bacon strips onto non-stick grill pan and into oven for 20 minutes or until desired doneness is reached. Remove from oven and set aside to cool slightly. Brush bacon with bourbon reduction and place back in oven for 5–10 minutes to caramelized reduction onto bacon.

7. Place burger patties onto griddle. Dust with burger seasoning and lightly drizzle with steak seasoning. Cover with griddle press for 10 seconds, then cook for 10 minutes per side to develop crust on the burger. Place American cheese slices onto burgers. Cover with melting dome until cheese is gooey. Remove burgers to resting pan.

8. In a bowl, combine mayonnaise, mustard, ketchup, BBQ sauce, and Bloody Mary mix. Stir until combined.

9. In a small bowl, melt 4 tablespoons salted butter. Brush each brioche bun with butter. Place on griddle, watching closely until the buns are a light golden brown, then set aside until you're ready to construct your burgers.

10. To construct these wonderful burgers, begin by spreading condiment mixture on the top and bottom buns. Place pickle chips, followed by the two burger patties covered in melted American cheese. Place bourbon reduction bacon on top, followed by the caramelized onions and the top bun. Anchor it all together with a burger skewer.

"*Cooking is like snow skiing: If you don't fall at least 10 times, then you're not skiing hard enough.*"

—Guy Fieri

The Sloppy Ho

Head Cook:
Andrea Woolf

Team Name:
Tucker Meat Market
Clarkston, GA

Business Name:
Tucker Meat Market

Facebook:
Tucker Meat Market

Instagram:
@TuckerMeatMarket

www.TuckerMeatMarket.com

A vegetarian burger (Impossible burger) that is skillfully layered with a beer cheese sauce, a beer infused tomato-onion jam, dill pickles, and onion.

Cook Time: 45 Minutes I Makes 4–6 servings

Ingredients

TOMATO ONION JAM:

4 onions, diced

4 tomatoes, diced

2 teaspoons brown sugar

8 teaspoons granulated sweetener (I used Pyure Organic Granulated Sweetener)

1 cup beer (I used Boulevard Brewing Tank 7)

4 tablespoons apple cider vinegar

1 teaspoon crushed red pepper

1 tablespoon salt

1 tablespoon black pepper

8 tablespoons olive oil

AMERICAN SAISON BEER CHEESE SAUCE:

6 tablespoons flour

6 tablespoons butter

1 cup heavy cream

2 cups milk

2 teaspoons salt

2 teaspoons black pepper

1¾ cup beer (I used Boulevard Brewing Tank 7)

6 tablespoons spicy mustard

4 teaspoons onion powder

4 teaspoons garlic powder

2 teaspoons cayenne pepper

2 9-ounce blocks of fontina cheese, shredded

BURGERS:

Pretzel buns

4 teaspoons zesty seasoning of your choice

1½ pounds plant-based meat (I used Impossible Burger meat)

Dill pickles

1 onion, sliced

Directions

1. Add zesty seasoning to plant-based meat and set aside.

TOMATO ONION JAM:

1. Heat olive oil in saucepan and sauté onions until soft and caramelized.
2. Stir in black pepper.
3. Add diced tomatoes and sugars, and sauté tomatoes until they're soft and starting to break down. Smash mixture with spoon.
4. Add the beer, vinegar, salt, and crushed red pepper. Bring to a boil.

5. Boil for 10 minutes, then reduce to a simmer for 10 minutes. Remove from heat.

AMERICAN SAISON BEER CHEESE SAUCE:

1. Melt butter in saucepan, whisk flour in, and cook for 5 minutes.
2. Slowly whisk in beer and milk until combined. Bring to boil until it starts to thicken.
3. Add heavy cream, fontina cheese, mustard, garlic powder, cayenne, onion powder, salt, and pepper. Once combined, stir until melted.

BURGERS:

1. Grill burger patties until fully cooked (no longer pink) then assemble.

ASSEMBLY:

1. Bottom bun
2. Tomato onion jam
3. Pickle
4. Burger
5. Beer cheese sauce
6. Sliced onion
7. Top bun

"Food should be fun."
—Thomas Keller

Head Cook:
Tommy Shive

Team Name:
Team Shive
Memphis, TN

Facebook:
Tommy Shive

Let your tastebuds enjoy the combination of flavors layered in this Surf'N'Turf Burger. This burger features an El Chupacabra Chop Haus seasoned Wagyu patty, served over a roasted jalapeño cream cheese, sweet green crisp lettuce, then topped with shredded Asadero cheese, crispy seasoned fried shrimp, Bangin' sauce, fresh made pico de gallo, and avocado lime creme, served on made-from-scratch hamburger buns. The inspiration behind this dish was to do a twist of a classic Surf'N'Turf dinner, but instead of steak and lobster, I used ground beef and fried shrimp as the protein components of the dish. Fried shrimp is one of my favorite dishes that my mother used to cook for me growing up and I wanted to find a way to use it on a burger in competition. Enjoy!

Prep Time: 20 Minutes | Cook Time: 15 Minutes | Makes 6 servings

Ingredients

ROASTED JALAPEÑO CREAM CHEESE:

4 ounces whipped cream cheese

1½ jalapeños

FRESH PICO DE GALLO:

1 cup seeded and chopped tomato

½ cup seeded and chopped jalapeño

1 cup chopped red onion

1 tablespoon minced garlic

½ cup vinegar

½ cup lime juice

Salt, to taste

¼ cup chopped cilantro

BANGIN' SAUCE:

½ cup mayonnaise

¼ cup sweet chili sauce

1 tablespoon honey

¼ teaspoon hot chili sauce

AVOCADO LIME CREMA:

2 avocados, peeled and diced

1 cup Mexican crema

Juice of ½ lime

Salt and pepper, to taste

CLASSIC FRIED SHRIMP:

½ cup milk

1 egg, beaten

1 cup all-purpose flour

3–4 tablespoons all-purpose seasoning (I used 2 Gringos Chupacabra Special Blend)

1 tablespoon smoked paprika

1 tablespoon black pepper

1 tablespoon salt

QUICK BUNS:
(YIELDS 6 BUNS)

2 tablespoons fast rise yeast

½ cup warm water (temp 95°F–105°F)

½ cup beer (temp 95°F–105°F)

⅓ cup vegetable oil

¼ cup sugar

1 large egg, beaten

1 teaspoon salt

2 tablespoons frozen butter, grated

¼ cup milk powder

3–3½ cups bread flour

BURGERS:

2 pounds ground American Wagyu

All-purpose seasoning, to taste (I used 2 Gringos El Chupacabra Chop Haus Blend)

TIPS:

- You can substitute these Quick Buns with brioche buns.

- You can substitute Wagyu ground beef with ground top ribeye steak or any other ground heavily marbled meat with a high fat content.

Directions

ROASTED JALAPEÑO CREAM CHEESE:

1. Preheat oven to 350°F.
2. Roast jalapeños for 10 minutes. When cool, finely chop the jalapeños.
3. Combine with whipped cream cheese and leave at room temperature until ready to serve.

FRESH PICO DE GALLO:

1. Combine tomato, jalapeño, minced garlic, and red onion.
2. Add equal amounts of vinegar and lime juice and stir well to combine.
3. Salt to taste. Add chopped cilantro.

4. Place in fridge until ready to serve.

BANGIN' SAUCE:

1. Combine all ingredients.
2. Cover and set aside.

AVOCADO LIME CREMA:

1. Blend all ingredients (except salt and pepper).
2. Add salt and pepper to taste.

CLASSIC FRIED SHRIMP:

1. In a bowl, combine egg and milk.
2. In another bowl, combine flour and the next 5 ingredients.

3. Heat the oil in a heavy-duty skillet (about 3–4 inches deep, or your deep-fryer to 350°F). If you don't have a thermometer, test by tossing a pinch of flour onto the hot oil...if it sinks and doesn't sizzle, it's not ready. If it browns too quickly, it's too hot.
4. Working in batches, use a slotted spoon to remove the shrimp from the egg/milk mixture and transfer to the seasoned flour. Using a separate dry spoon (or your fingers), toss to evenly coat.
5. Carefully slip the battered shrimp into the hot oil and fry until golden brown and crisp, about 4 minutes.

"Cooking requires confident guesswork and improvisation—experimentation and substitution, dealing with failure and uncertainty in a creative way."

—Paul Theroux

DIRECTIONS CONTINUED

6. Drain on paper towels. Once shrimp have drained, transfer to a large bowl.

QUICK BUNS:

1. Preheat oven to 400°–415°F.

2. In a large bowl, dissolve yeast in warm water/beer, oil, and sugar and let stand for about 5 minutes.

3. In a separate bowl, combine flour, milk powder, and salt and whisk together. Add grated butter and use fingers to work into flour mixture.

4. Add beaten egg to the yeast mixture and lightly whisk.

5. Add flour mixture to wet ingredients and mix well to make a soft dough. You want the dough to be sticky, but workable. Add more flour as needed.

6. Turn dough onto a floured surface. Knead by hand until smooth and elastic, about 6–8 minutes.

7. Grease bowl and place dough back in bowl and cover with a towel. Let rise 10–15 minutes.

8. Turn dough back onto floured surface and knead to remove most air.

9. Divide and shape into balls and place on baking sheet. Cover with towel to rise 15 minutes.

10. Brush with a beaten egg. Bake for 8–12 minutes or until golden brown. Remove from pans to wire rack to cool.

11. Cut in half, brush with butter, and broil in oven until desired color/toasted.

BURGERS:

1. Roll meat into 5½-ounce balls.

2. Press into a patty then season meat liberally on both sides.

3. Preheat grill to 375°F. Place patties on and grill for 5–6 minutes.

4. Flip and grill for another 4 minutes.

5. Add shredded cheese to top of burger and let melt for next 2 minutes.

6. Remove from grill to a pan and let rest for 2 minutes.

ASSEMBLY:

1. Place bottom toasted bun on plate with ½ tablespoon of jalapeño cream cheese spread across top.

2. Top jalapeño cream cheese with lettuce.

3. Place burger patties with melted cheese on top of lettuce.

4. Top with 4–5 fried shrimp.

5. Drizzle Bangin' Sauce across top of shrimp.

6. Top shrimp with ½ tablespoon of fresh pico.

7. Brush bottom side of top bun with avocado lime crema.

8. Skewer and place top bun onto top of build.

This burger consists of a Texan Wagyu minced steak seasoned with Brisket Magic spices, featuring a homemade relish sauce, fried onion "doughnuts" with popcorn and cornflakes breadcrumbs, minced iceberg salad, a minute compote of sweet onions, crushed roasted pecans, and smoked bacon. Lightly decorated with homemade chipotle ketchup.

Cook Time: 1 Hour, 30 Minutes | Makes 6 servings

Ingredients

PECAN AND POPCORN BUNS:

3 cups flour Type 55

¼ cup pecans

¼ cup popcorn

1 8.75-ounce can corn

5 ounces potatoes

1 ounce baker's yeast

1 pasteurized egg

1½ cups semi-skimmed milk

1 ounce butter

1 ounce olive oil

RELISH SAUCE:

1¾ cups apple cider vinegar

⅛ cup cane sugar

2½ cups water

1 tablespoon turmeric

2 tablespoons honey

2 sprigs dill

1 tablespoon mustard

1 sweet onion, minced

1 cucumber, minced

4 small pickles, minced

1 dozen okras, minced

3 jalapeños, minced

3 cactus leaves

PORK BELLY:

12 slices bacon

All-purpose seasoning, to taste (I used 2 Gringos Chupacabra Special Blend)

2 tablespoons honey

2 tablespoons bourbon

FRIED ONION DOUGHNUTS:

X vegetable oil

2 large sweet onions, thinly sliced

¼ cup cornflakes

¼ cup popcorn

1 cup flour

One 12-ounce can beer

MEAT:

1½ pound ground beef

7 ounces butter

Brisket rub, to taste (I used 2 Gringos Chupacabra Brisket Magic)

HOT SAUCE:

¾ cup minced onions

3 heads garlic, minced

1 tablespoon all-purpose seasoning (I used 2 Gringos Chupacabra Special Blend)

7 ounces raspberries

3½ ounces blueberries

3½ ounces blackberries

3 small chipotle peppers, minced

1 tablespoon Worcestershire sauce

2 tablespoons brown sugar

1 tablespoon hot sauce, or to taste (I used El Yucateco Black Label Reserve Chile Habanero Hot Sauce)

GARLIC BURGER SAUCE:

1 cup mayonnaise

⅓ cup mustard

1 teaspoon smoked paprika

2 tablespoons poultry seasoning (I used 2 Gringos Chupacabra Chuckalicious Spices)

3 heads garlic, minced

BURGERS:

1 head iceberg lettuce, chopped

6 ounces cheddar cheese, sliced (I used Tillamook County Creamery Association Special Reserve Cheddar)

6 ounces smoked cheddar cheese, sliced (I used Carr Valley Apple Smoked Cheddar)

Vegetable oil

OTHER INGREDIENTS:

Hot sauce, to taste (I used El Yucateco Green Chile Habanero Hot Sauce)

7 ounces soda (I used Dr. Pepper)

7 ounces port wine

Head Cook:
Thibaud Desimeur

Team Name:
Team Burger France
Saint Pierre des Corps, France

Business Name:
Le Tatoué Toqué

Facebook:
Le Tatoué Toqué

Instagram:
@lttresto

www.LeTatoueToque.fr

"Food is memories."

—José Andrés

Directions

PECAN AND POPCORN BUNS:

1. Preheat the oven to 370°F. Heat skillet and pop popcorn over high heat.

2. Roast the pecans in the oven. Once roasted, coarsely chop them.

3. In a bowl, purée potatoes, corn, and baker's yeast.

4. Add the mixture to a stand mixer with the flour and stir for 5 minutes.

5. Add the egg and stir.

6. Add the butter and oil and stir until the dough comes away from the wall.

7. Divide the dough into pieces and let it rise for 30 minutes.

8. Add the egg wash, crushed popcorn, and roasted pecans nuts and cook for 15 minutes at 370°F.

RELISH SAUCE

1. In a saucepan over medium heat, mix apple cider vinegar, cane sugar, and water.

2. Add turmeric, honey, dill, and yellow mustard. Bring to a boil.

3. Bring a separate pot of water to a boil.

4. Clean the okras, pickles, cucumbers, jalapeños, and sweet onions and mince. Place all in a bowl and toss.

5. Remove the thorns from the cactus and immerse leaves in pot of boiling water for 7 minutes.

6. Once the mixture is brought to a boil, remove from the heat and then pour into bowl containing the vegetables.

7. Leave to infuse and set aside for dressing.

PORK BELLY:

1. Arrange the bacon slices on parchment paper.

2. Season with all-purpose seasoning and bourbon honey.

3. Bake at 355°F for 10 minutes, then take them out and let rest.

4. Bake again for 10 minutes just before cooking the steaks. Reserve for dressage.

FRIED ONION DOUGHNUTS:

1. Preheat a pan with vegetable oil to 355°F.

2. Cut the onions into thin strips.

3. Mix cornflakes, special blend spice, and popcorn to make "homemade breadcrumbs."

4. In a separate bowl, make a doughnut batter with equal parts flour and beer.

5. Dip the onions in the doughnut batter first, then dip into the breadcrumb mixture.

6. Fry until they reach a golden-brown color.

7. Take them out and place them on absorbent paper to remove excess fat. Reserve it for dressage.

MEAT:

1. Form 8 balls of 3 ounces. Refrigerate.

2. Mix butter with the brisket rub mixture. Form a sausage and keep it cool.

HOT SAUCE:

1. In a saucepan, brown the onions and garlic over high heat.

2. Once colored, add seasoning, then add in the raspberries, blueberries, blackberries, chipotle peppers, Worcestershire sauce, and brown sugar. Allow to reduce.

3. Once the mixture obtains a ketchup-like texture, strain through a cheesecloth.

4. Return to saucepan, reduce heat, and add hot sauce.

5. Mix well and put in a pipette for dressing.

GARLIC BURGER SAUCE:

1. Combine ingredients and set aside until ready to assemble burger.

COOKING AND DRESSING:

1. Finely chop the iceberg lettuce and thinly slice the two types of cheddar cheese.

2. Take the meat out of the fridge.

3. Using clean hands, pat and roll out 3-ounce balls to form a patty shape.

4. Cut slices of previously prepared butter.

5. Place a disc of butter on top of each of the patties. Close with another patty until you have formed a very compact steak.

6. Cook the meat on both sides at 300°F with a little vegetable oil until you get a nice crust.

7. Move the meat to one side of the griddle where it's less hot at 150°F, brushing each side with the butter mixture.

8. Two minutes before taking out the steaks, place the slices of cheddar and bacon on top.

9. At the same time, toast the buns until a "crust" is obtained, which will prevent the bun from soaking up too much sauce and juice.

10. At the same time, make the sweet onions with the reduced stock made from the waste.

ASSEMBLY:

1. Arrange the lower part of the bun on the plate.

2. Spread a thin layer of sauce on the bun. Add a little iceberg lettuce on top.

3. Place the steak with the cheddar and bacon on top.

4. Add the sweet onions.

5. On the top bun, add a nice layer of sauce and lay the iceberg and roasted pecans.

6. Add fried onions and close the top of the bun. The burger is ready to eat!

The Ultimate Double Mushroom Bacon Swiss Burger was made with fresh ground Wagyu chuck, Swiss cheese, sauteed mushrooms with bacon, a creamy garlic aioli, and topped with crispy onion straws, all served on a toasted classic, all-American burger bun. The bun I used was from Nobel Bread, a local Phoenix, AZ bakery—the Fudd Bun.

Prep Time: 45 Minutes | Cook Time: 30 Minutes | Makes 6 servings

Head Cook:
Rick Muterspaugh

Team Name:
Rick Muterspaugh
Phoenix, AZ

Business Name:
Retired after 40 years with
Burger King

Facebook:
Rick.Muterspaugh.7

Instagram:
@RickMuterspaugh

Twitter:
@BBQRam

Ingredients

MUSHROOMS:

48 ounces baby bella mushrooms

5 tablespoons butter

4 garlic cloves, minced

4 teaspoons black garlic umami sauce

2 tablespoons Worcestershire sauce

1 teaspoon umami seasoning (I used Trader Joe's Mushroom & Company Umami Seasoning Blend)

CREAMY GARLIC AIOLI:

¾ cup mayonnaise

3 garlic cloves, minced

2½ tablespoons fresh lemon juice

Salt and pepper, to taste

ONION STRAWS:

3 large yellow onions

4 cups buttermilk

2 quarts canola oil

3 cups all-purpose flour

3 teaspoons garlic powder

1 teaspoon onion powder

1½ teaspoons umami seasoning (I used Trader Joe's Mushroom & Company Umami Seasoning Blend)

1½ teaspoons paprika

1½ teaspoons cayenne pepper

1½ teaspoons chili powder

Salt and pepper, to taste

BURGERS:

3 pounds Wagyu ground beef

2 tablespoons salt

1 tablespoon pepper

3 tablespoons garlic powder

¼ cup Worcestershire sauce

Seasoning mixture (I used 2 parts 2 Gringos Chupacabra Brisket Magic to 1 part Gringos Chupacabra Fine Meat Rub)

6 burger buns

24 slices Swiss cheese

1 pound bacon

4 tablespoons Wagyu beef tallow

TIPS:

- You can substitute Wagyu ground beef with ground top ribeye steak or any other ground heavily marbled meat with a high fat content.

- You can substitute Wagyu beef tallow with regular beef tallow.

Directions

1. Put ground beef in a bowl and mix with salt, pepper, garlic powder, and bloom Worcestershire sauce. Divide the beef into 12 3-ounce balls. Roll the balls in the seasoning mixture and flatten into a patty. **Note:** I used a tortilla press to make my patties thin and slightly larger than the bun.

2. Wash mushrooms and add to a large skillet. Sauté mushrooms, adding the butter, garlic, bloom sauce, black garlic umami sauce, and umami seasoning.

3. Chop bacon into small pieces and cook in a cast-iron skillet. Drain grease and set bacon aside. Add to mushroom mixture when ready.

4. Prepare garlic aioli by mixing all ingredients together and set aside.

5. Pour canola oil into a large pan or fryer for frying onion straws. Heat to 350°F.

6. Slice onions using a mandolin (setting 2). Soak onion slices in buttermilk for 30 minutes.

7. Add spices and ingredients to all-purpose flour in a one gallon Ziploc bag or large foil pan.

8. Remove onion slices from the buttermilk, coat with flour mixture, and fry in oil at 350°F until crisp. Remove from fryer, pat with paper towels, and add salt to onion straws.

9. Cook formed patties on griddle or cast-iron skillet using small amount of Wagyu beef tallow. Season with salt and pepper upon turning and add two slices of Swiss cheese for each patty.

10. Toast buns on griddle or skillet.

ASSEMBLY:

1. Bottom bun

2. Garlic aioli

3. Two patties with cheese, mushroom and bacon mixture

4. Onion straws

5. Garlic aioli

6. Top bun

"I love to compete, meet new people, and share ideas, concepts, and recipes. Most of all, I love to see people enjoy the food I prepare."

—Rick Muterspaugh

Blackberry Bleu

Head Cook:
Aaron Bradshaw

Team Name:
Crissy's Pub Style
Benton, AR

Business Name:
Crissy's Pub Style

Facebook:
Crissy's Pub Style

Instagram:
@Crissys2022

A prime beef patty topped with a blackberry bourbon sauce, bleu cheese crumbles, and hickory smoked bacon on a brioche bun dressed with spicy brown mustard, green leaf lettuce, Roma tomatoes, and sliced red onion.

Cook Time: 1 Hour | Makes 8 servings

Ingredients

BURGERS:

3 pounds ground sirloin

1 pound ground chuck

2 teaspoons Cajun seasoning

Ancho chili powder, to taste

16 slices bacon

Green leaf lettuce

Bleu cheese crumbles

Roma tomato slices (2 per burger)

Red onion slices (2 per burger)

1 teaspoon spicy brown mustard (per burger)

8 brioche buns (I used Member's Mark)

24 slices Swiss cheese

1 pound bacon

4 tablespoons Wagyu beef tallow

BLACKBERRY BOURBON SAUCE:

2 tablespoons butter

2 tablespoons olive oil

⅛ cup chopped red onion

2 cloves garlic, chopped

1 teaspoon red pepper flakes

1½ cups fresh blackberries

2 tablespoons balsamic vinegar

Juice from 1 lemon

¼ cup water

1 tablespoon brown sugar

2 13-ounce jars blackberry preserves (I used Bonne Maman)

2 tablespoons unsalted butter

2 ounces bourbon (I used Rock Town Bourbon)

⅛ cup water

Directions

BACON:

1. Preheat oven to 350°F.
2. Place bacon on sheet pans and into the oven for approximately 40 minutes or until desired texture.

BURGER SEASONING:

1. 1. Combine Cajun seasoning and ancho chili powder in spice grinder to blend thoroughly set aside for later.

BLACKBERRY BOURBON SAUCE:

1. Heat butter and olive oil and begin to sauté the chopped red onion.
2. As the edges of the onions begin to change color, add the chopped garlic.

3. Allow to begin turning golden before adding red pepper flakes, balsamic vinegar, and the fresh blackberries.
4. Allow to cook down, then add the blackberry preserves, lemon juice, and water. Simmer until desired consistency.
5. Add bourbon and burn off excess alcohol.
6. Remove from heat and allow to cool before placing in food processor on high for about a minute. Pour into squeeze bottle for later.

BUNS:

1. Butter the brioche buns and lightly toast.

BURGERS:

1. Ball 8 ounces ground sirloin and ground chuck in a 3:1 sirloin to chuck ratio and allow to chill.
2. When ready, roll the meat ball in reserved seasoning and smash on hot griddle until ready to flip.
3. Add the Blackberry Bourbon Sauce and crumbled bleu cheese and allow to melt, removing from the heat and setting aside to rest.
4. Place on bottom bun.
5. Top each burger with 2 slices of bacon.
6. Add spicy brown mustard, green leaf lettuce, Roma tomato slices, and red onion slices to top bun.
7. Enjoy!

"Food may not be the answer to world peace, but it's a start."

—Anthony Bourdain

Head Cook:
Andrea Woolf

Team Name:
Tucker Meat Market
Clarkston, GA

Business Name:
Tucker Meat Market

Facebook:
Tucker Meat Market

Instagram:
@TuckerMeatMarket

www.TuckerMeatMarket.com

Cook Time: 1 Hour | Makes 8 servings

Ingredients

KIMCHI SLAW:

1–2 pounds napa cabbage, sliced/shredded

¼ cup hot pepper flakes

1 tablespoon sugar

¼ cup fish sauce

4 tablespoons garlic paste

3 green onions, sliced

1 carrot, thinly sliced/shredded

1 pickled daikon radish, sliced

GARLIC SOY MARINATED PORK BELLY:

1½ pounds thin slice pork belly

6–8 tsp garlic paste

2 tablespoons sesame oil

2 tablespoons miso

1 tablespoon honey

¼ cup soy sauce

1 tablespoon ginger paste

BURGER PATTIES:

2 pounds bacon burger blend

2 slices bread

¼ cup grated onion

2 tablespoons honey

2 tablespoons sugar

½ cup puréed Asian pear

1½ teaspoons black pepper

2 tablespoons water

1 green onion, chopped

2 cloves garlic, minced

1 teaspoon salt

1 teaspoon ginger paste

½ cup diced green onion

KOREAN AIOLI:

1 cup mayonnaise

2 tablespoons gochujang

6 eggs

ADDITIONAL INGREDIENTS:

1 head green lettuce

Green onion buns

Directions

KIMCHI SLAW:

1. Soak sliced/shredded napa cabbage in a salt water brine and set aside.
2. Make the dressing by mixing hot pepper flakes, sugar, fish sauce, and garlic paste. Set aside.
3. After 30 minutes, drain and rinse brined cabbage.
4. In a bowl, mix cabbage, green onion, and carrots with the kimchi dressing.
5. Blend in sliced pickled daikon radish.

GARLIC SOY MARINATED PORK BELLY:

1. Make marinade by mixing garlic paste, sesame oil, miso, honey, soy sauce, and ginger paste.
2. Pour mixture over pork belly then set aside for 30 to 40 minutes.
3. Grill on a flat top or pan with a little oil.

BURGER PATTIES:

1. Make bulgogi marinade by mixing grated onion, honey, sugar, puréed Asian pear, ½ teaspoon black pepper, water, and green onion.
2. Once marinade is made, break up the bread into a bowl. Add ¼ cup of the marinade to the bread and break down the bread as much as possible.
3. Add the bacon burger blend, minced garlic, 1 teaspoon black pepper, salt, ginger paste, and diced green onion and blend together.
4. Form into patties and grill to desired doneness basting with the extra marinade.

KOREAN AIOLI:

1. Mix together mayonnaise and gochujang.
2. Fry eggs to over medium.

ASSEMBLY:

1. Slice and toast the buns.
2. Top with aioli, green lettuce, burger patty, garlic pork belly, fried egg, kimchi slaw, and more aioli on top of the bun.

"Chefs don't make mistakes; they make new dishes."

—Elizabeth Brigg

the
BACON

Head Cook:
Jonathan Giovannoni

Team Name:
Team Jonathan G
Miami, FL

Business Name:
One Oak Kitchen

Facebook:
Jonathan.Giovannoni

Instagram:
@OneOakKitchen and
@NextGenerationCatering

www.OneOakKitchen.com

A crispy and flaky cannoli shell filled with smoky bacon, mascarpone, and ricotta mousse. Served on a bed of dark chocolate and smoked bacon lardon soil, caramelized banana and a bourbon peach and bacon chutney. Paired with fresh seasonal fruits, herbs, and flowers.

Cook Time: 1 Hour, 15 Minutes | Makes 4–6 servings

Ingredients

MASCARPONE & RICOTTA MOUSSE/CANNOLI FILLING:

4–6 cannoli shells

4⅓ cups + 2 tablespoons mascarpone cheese (full fat)

5 cups + 2 tablespoons ricotta cheese, drained

1½ cups white sugar

15¾ ounces hickory smoked sliced bacon, fully cooked (I used Pederson's Natural Farms)

BOURBON PEACH & BACON CHUTNEY:

1½ cups + 1 tablespoon canned peaches

4¼ ounces bacon lardons, cooked and strained of fat

2 ounces apple cider vinegar

2 tablespoons + 1 teaspoon maple syrup

⅔ cup peach tea (I used Lipton)

1 teaspoon agar-agar

1 ounce bourbon

DARK CHOCOLATE & SMOKED BACON LARDON SOIL:

7 ounces dark chocolate, 70%

2¼ cups white sugar

5¾ ounces water

⅓ cup + 2 tablespoons Dutch-process cocoa powder

10½ ounces bacon, cooked and strained of fat

CARAMELIZED BANANAS:

2 medium bananas

½ cup white sugar

SEASONAL FRUIT:

½ cup kumquats, seeded

½ cup raspberries

½ cup blackberries

½ cup black figs

½ cup pomegranate

GARNISH:

Mint leaves

1 tablespoon matcha powder

½ cup powdered sugar

Smoked sea salt

Directions

CRUMBLED BACON:

1. Preheat oven to 400°F.
2. Place sliced bacon on two cookie sheets and cook in oven until crispy.
3. Remove from oven, strain oil, and pat dry with paper towel.
4. Use a knife to slice into thin slivers and then cut into crumbs. Set aside in a bowl lined with paper towels for cannoli garnish.

MASCARPONE & RICOTTA MOUSSE/CANNOLI FILLING:

1. In a large bowl, combine ricotta, mascarpone, and sugar. Use an electric mixer to blend until smooth and fluffy.
2. Cut 4 pounds, 6½ ounces bacon into lardons and place in large pot to cook.
3. Strain bacon on stove and place back on heat to crisp. Set aside on paper towel to drain.
4. Add crumbled bacon to ricotta mixture. Use immersion blender to blend until no large lumps appear.

5. Place in piping bag with tip. Set aside.

BOURBON PEACH & BACON CHUTNEY:

1. In a medium pot, add peaches, apple cider vinegar, maple syrup, peach tea, and agar-agar. Cook for 15 minutes on medium heat.
2. Add cooked bacon and cook until thickened.
3. Blend using immersion blender, then set aside.

DARK CHOCOLATE & SMOKED BACON LARDON SOIL:

1. In a large pot, place water and sugar to boil, cook until 135° F.
2. Add the dark chocolate and cocoa powder. Mix until thickened.
3. Dump mixture onto cookie sheet lined with baking mat. Allow to cool.
4. Break hardened mixture into small crumbs.

5. Add crumbled bacon to mix and set aside.

CARAMELIZED BANANAS:

1. Slice bananas into slices, coat with sugar, and bake until slightly golden.
2. Remove from oven and set aside.

FRUIT:

1. Cut all decorative fruits into halves. Set aside.
2. Remove pit from pomegranate seeds. Set aside.

ASSEMBLY:

1. Place chocolate soil on bottom of dish.
2. Fill cannoli shell with mascarpone/ricotta filling.
3. Dip into bacon crumbs, place over soil.
4. Decorate soil with assorted cut fruits, peach jam, and brûléed bananas.
5. Garnish with mint leaves, smoked sea salt, matcha powder, and powdered sugar.

"You can't cook if you don't like people."

—Joël Robuchon

Acorn Squash Stuffed with Bacon and Fall Vegetables

Head Cook:
Peter Radjou

Team Name:
Radjou's
Roanoke, VA

This recipe utilizes the bountiful freshly harvested vegetables of the fall. It was created at a farmers market inspired by the beautiful seasonal produce. It won Chef Radjou the "Bacon World Food Championship" in 2018.

Prep Time: 30 Minutes | Cook Time: 1 Hour | Makes 4–6 servings

Ingredients

- 3 acorn squash
- 1 small butternut squash, peeled and diced
- 1 pound bacon
- 1 14-ounce can of petite diced tomatoes (I used Red Gold Tomatoes with Green Chilies)
- ½ carrot, peeled and diced
- ½ red onion, diced
- 3 garlic cloves, chopped

- ½ red pepper, diced
- 1 small zucchini, diced
- 1 small yellow squash, diced
- 1 teaspoon rosemary, chopped
- ½ stick butter
- 1 tablespoon brown sugar
- 8 ounces Gruyère cheese, grated
- ½ cup heavy cream
- 2 tablespoons all-purpose flour
- ¼ cup white wine

- Black pepper, to taste
- Salt, to taste
- ¼ teaspoon crushed red pepper flakes
- 4 ounces grated parmesan cheese
- Beet puree, for plate decoration and garnish
- Rosemary sprigs, for garnish

Directions

1. Cut acorn squash into halves and scoop out the seeds.
2. Combine melted butter, brown sugar, and salt and brush it on the inside of the acorn squash. Reserve the rest of the butter mixture. Roast acorn squash in the oven on 350°F for 30 minutes.
3. Combine diced butternut squash with remaining brown sugar and butter mixture and layer it on a greased tray and cook in the oven until tender.
4. Chop bacon and cook in a sauté pan, strain, and reserve.
5. Return half of the bacon fat to the pan and sauté diced onion until translucent.
6. Add garlic and carrot and cook to tender.
7. Add all-purpose flour and cook.
8. Deglaze with white wine and add petite diced tomatoes infused with green chilies.
9. Add red pepper, zucchini, and squash.
10. Add chopped rosemary and season with crushed red pepper, black pepper, and salt.
11. Add cooked butternut squash, heavy cream, and half of the reserved cooked bacon.
12. Cook until it thickens.
13. Remove from the stovetop and add half of the grated Gruyère cheese and scoop the mixture into the roasted acorn squash.
14. Top with the remaining Gruyère cheese and grated parmesan.
15. Bake until the cheese is melted and bubbly. Garnish with the remaining crispy bacon.
16. Serve on a platter decorated with fall colors, such as beet puree.

"Always cook with fresh ingredients and don't forget to garnish with a sprinkle of love."

—Peter Radjou

Head Cook:
Peter Radjou

Team Name:
Radjou's
Roanoke, VA

This recipe was inspired by Chef Radjou's love for Cajun cooking. This dish is a take on a deconstructed authentic New Orleans gumbo. Chef's favorite element of this dish is the incorporation of seafood with bacon.

Prep Time: 30 Minutes | Cook Time: 1 Hour | Makes 4–6 servings

Ingredients

CRAB CAKE:
1 pound crab meat
1 pound bacon
½ onion, chopped
3 cloves garlic, chopped
1 small green bell pepper, chopped
1 stalk celery, chopped
1 tablespoon all-purpose flour
½ cup water
½ cup tomato sauce (I used Red Gold Chili Ready)
½ tablespoon Cajun seasoning
2 eggs

½ cup mayonnaise
4 slices white bread, diced
¼ cup panko breadcrumbs

BISQUE:
½ pound bacon
½ onion, chopped
2 cloves garlic, chopped
1 14-ounce can tomato sauce (I used Red Gold Chili Ready)
¼ teaspoon oregano
5 fresh basil leaves or ¼ teaspoon dried basil

½ teaspoon chili powder
¼ teaspoon crushed red pepper flakes
½ teaspoon black pepper
½ teaspoon cumin powder
½ teaspoon sugar
½ cup heavy cream

GARNISH:
3–4 okras
3 pieces asparagus
*Slice okra and asparagus diagonally and fry (or air fry) until crispy.

Directions

CRAB CAKE:
1. Preheat oven to 350°F.
2. Chop bacon and render the fat. Strain and reserve fat.
3. Chop the onion, garlic, and celery.
4. Sauté onion, garlic, green bell pepper, and celery with some of the reserved bacon fat. Add flour and cook to make a dark roux. Add water and tomato sauce and Cajun seasoning. Cook until it thickens.
5. Transfer into a bowl, cool it slightly and then add eggs, mayonnaise, diced white bread, panko breadcrumbs, cooked bacon, and crab meat.
6. Mix it together and make cakes of the desired size and quantity.
7. In a heavy-duty skillet, add reserved bacon fat and shallow fry the crab cakes until golden brown.

BISQUE:
1. Chop bacon and render the fat. Strain and reserve bacon.
2. Chop the onion and garlic. Sauté in bacon fat and cook until translucent.
3. Add tomato sauce and season with fresh basil, oregano, chili powder, crushed red pepper, cumin powder, and black pepper. Bring it to a boil and taste for seasoning and add salt if needed.
4. Cool it slightly and transfer to a blender and blend until smooth.
5. Strain and bring it to a boil in a saucepan and add heavy cream.
6. Season with sugar.
7. To serve, fill the plate with tomato bisque and the crab cake on top.
8. And chopped, cooked, reserved bacon on the bisque.
9. Garnish with crispy asparagus and okra.

"Always cook from your heart and cook unique, keeping in mind who you're cooking for."

—Peter Radjou

Bacon and Tomato Ménage á Trois

Head Cook:
Stephen Coe

Team Name:
COE-LANE
Plymouth, VA

Business Name:
Lobsta Love Food Truck

Facebook:
Chef Stephen Coe

Instagram:
@ChefStephenCoe

www.ChefStephenCoe.com

Bacon wrapped bacon, lollipop bacon chop, bacon and sweet potato hash, tomato bacon jam, bacon and tomato bearnaise, tomato and brown butter vinaigrette.

Cook Time: 1 Hour 30 Minutes | Makes 4–6 servings

Ingredients

BACON TOMATO BÉARNAISE:

2 slices thick cut bacon, minced

½ medium onion, minced

½ cup diced tomatoes (I used Reds Gold Diced Tomatoes with Green Chilies)

2 sticks butter

3 large egg yolks

1 tablespoon sherry vinegar

2 dashes Worcestershire sauce

1 teaspoon fresh tarragon

BACON AND SWEET POTATO HASH:

Extra-virgin olive oil, for the pan

1½ pounds sweet potatoes, peeled and cut into ½-inch cubes

12 ounces thick cut bacon, cut into lardons

1 jalapeño with stem, seeds, and ribs removed, cut into thin rings

Kosher salt and freshly ground black pepper, to taste

¼ cup freshly chopped cilantro

1 cup demi

¼ cup sherry vinegar

PORK BELLY:

12 ounces pork belly

6 slices bacon

2 tablespoons butter

1 teaspoon Herbes de Provence

Salt and pepper, to taste

TOMATO AND BACON JAM:

½ pound smoked bacon

1 can tomatoes, chopped (I used Red Gold Canned Diced Tomatoes)

1 yellow sweet onion, finely diced

1 cup white sugar

2½ tablespoons apple cider vinegar

1½ teaspoons salt

¼ teaspoon black pepper

1 dash hot pepper sauce (I used Frank's RedHot)

LOLLIPOP BACON CHOP:

3-pound rack bone-in bacon

½ cup water

2 tablespoons Dijon mustard

2 teaspoons butter, at room temperature

½ teaspoon salt

½ teaspoon pepper

½ teaspoon Herbes de Provence

Directions

BACON TOMATO BÉARNAISE:

1. Place minced bacon in a small fry pan over medium heat to render its fat and make crispy.

2. While the bacon is cooking, melt the butter in a pot over low heat for 10 minutes.

3. Place the egg yolks in a blender along with vinegar, diced tomatoes, tarragon, hot bacon, and bacon fat. Blend until smooth.

4. With the blender running on slow, pour the now-clarified butter into the container, leaving the milk solids in the bottom of the pot. The hot butter will cook the egg yolks.

BACON AND SWEET POTATO HASH:

1. Lay the cubed sweet potatoes in an even layer on the sheet pan. Roast until just tender, about 10 minutes. Set aside.

2. Meanwhile, add the bacon to a cast iron pan on medium heat. Cook until the bacon is crispy and the fat has rendered, about 7 minutes. Remove to a paper towel-lined plate and set aside.

3. Add the jalapeño rings to the bacon fat and fry until blistered and lightly browned. Transfer to the paper towel-lined plate with the bacon.

4. Turn the heat to medium-high. Add the cubed sweet potatoes in an even layer and season with cinnamon and some salt and pepper. Fry until crispy and golden brown on all sides, about 7 minutes.

5. Add the bacon and jalapeños to the pan and fold to combine. Add a few shakes of vinegar and demi. Transfer to a serving dish and garnish with cilantro.

PORK BELLY:

1. Wrap pork belly with thin bacon and render until crisp throughout.

2. Baste with butter and herbs.

TOMATO AND BACON JAM:

1. Cook the bacon in a large skillet over medium-high heat, turning occasionally until evenly browned, about 10 minutes. Drain the bacon slices on paper towels. Crumble bacon when cool.

2. Stir tomatoes, sweet onion, sugar, apple cider vinegar, salt, black pepper, and hot sauce together in a saucepan and bring to a boil, stirring constantly to dissolve sugar.

3. Stir in crumbled bacon and cook over medium heat, stirring often, until the spread is very thick, about 1 hour. Adjust salt and black pepper.

LOLLIPOP BACON CHOP:

1. Submerge bacon rack in a large saucepan filled with cold water. Cover with lid.

2. Bring to a boil, then turn heat down to a simmer. Cook for about 45 minutes to an hour and preheat oven to 450°F.

3. Remove bacon from the water and let cool a bit in a baking dish. Add ½ cup water to baking dish.

4. French and remove the rind and excess fat along a portion of the bone to create a lollipop handle.

5. In a small bowl, mix Dijon mustard, butter, salt, pepper, and Herbs de Provence. Spread over the fatty side of the bacon rack.

6. Place in the oven and cook at 450°F for 5 minutes. Then, turn oven down to 350°F and bake for another 15 minutes, or until golden brown.

"A recipe has no soul. You as the cook must bring soul to the recipe."

—Thomas Keller

Bacon Banana Split Bread Pudding
with Spiced Chocolate

Head Cook:
Staci Jett

Team Name:
Staci's Hog Heaven
Brooksville, KY

Business Name:
Custom Creations Catering

Facebook:
Staci Graves Jett

Instagram:
@fire_bourbon_and_bbq

Baked and pork fat grilled bacon-nut bread pudding stuffed with white chocolate and Italian black cherries on a bed of banana-bacon anglaise. Topped with bacon chili ganache, salted bourbon-caramel sauce, and peanut butter whipped cream. Garnished with candied mint, fresh banana, bacon bits, and thick-cut candied bacon covered with chocolate, almonds, and pistachios.

Cook Time: 1 Hour | Makes 4–6 servings

Ingredients

BACON NUT BREAD PUDDING:
2 pounds cubed brioche bread

3 cups heavy cream

2 cups milk

12 ounces butter

4 ounces pork fat

8 eggs

16 ounces sugar

½ teaspoon salt

1 tablespoon vanilla extract

1 vanilla bean

8 ounces black cherries

8 ounces candied almonds

½ pound bacon

¼ cup bacon grease

½ teaspoon ginger

BANANA-BACON ANGLAISE:
6 egg yolks

4 ounces sugar

1 cup milk

1 cup heavy cream

½ banana

1 vanilla bean

1 tablespoon bacon fat

SALTED BOURBON CARAMEL:
⅓ cup bourbon

2 cups brown sugar

1½ cups water

½ teaspoon salt

2 tablespoons unsalted butter

1 cup heavy cream

BACON CHILI GANACHE:
2 pounds chocolate (I used Hershey's)

2 cups heavy cream

2 teaspoons cayenne

2 teaspoons pork fat

PEANUT BUTTER WHIPPED CREAM:
2 cups heavy cream

2 tablespoons peanut butter

8 tablespoons powdered sugar

CANDIED CHOCOLATE BACON:
1 pound thick cut applewood smoked bacon

1 teaspoon black pepper

1 cup dark brown sugar

1/4 cup cinnamon sugar

Melted chocolate and white chocolate, for drizzle (I used Hershey's)

½ cup crushed pistachios

½ cup crushed almonds

OTHER:
20–25 whole mint leaves, for garnish

Directions

BACON NUT BREAD PUDDING:
1. Preheat the oven to 350°F.
2. In a skillet, cook bacon then remove when done, reserving the grease. Let bacon cool, crumble into small pieces, and set aside.
3. Bring the milk and cream to a boil then remove from heat.
4. Butter a baking dish and spread the cubed brioche in it.
5. Whisk the eggs, sugar, ginger, and salt together until bright and fluffy.
6. Temper with the hot milk, then mix in the bacon fat, butter, cherries, bacon, vanilla extract, vanilla pulp, and almonds.

7. Pour the custard over the brioche and bake the bread pudding for 20–25 minutes, or until the top is browned.
8. Let cool slightly.
9. Cut bread pudding discs out with cutter, then grill on each side for sixty seconds over pork fat.
10. Remove from heat and serve.

BANANA-BACON ANGLAISE:
1. Combine egg yolks and sugar and whip until bright and fluffy, then slowly whisk in bacon fat.
2. Scald milk and cream, but don't burn or boil.
3. In a thin stream, pour milk mixture into egg mixture, whisking continuously.

4. Once fully incorporated, stick bowl over simmering water and whisk consistently until thickened, but not overcooked.
5. Remove from heat and whisk in vanilla bean pulp once nappe consistency is reached.
6. Puree with 1/2 banana and return to mixing bowl, serve immediately.

SALTED BOURBON CARAMEL:
1. Place cream in a saucepan and bring to a boil, then leave over low heat.
2. Reduce bourbon to half volume on stove.
3. Bring sugar and water to a boil and let cook until golden/light brown in color.

DIRECTIONS CONTINUED

4. Remove sugar mixture from heat, and slowly whisk in heavy cream.

5. Whisk in butter and bourbon, then finish with salt until fully incorporated.

6. Simmer a bit more if thickening is necessary.

BACON CHILI GANACHE:

1. Place chocolate in a stainless steel bowl.

2. Bring heavy cream and pork fat to a simmer, then pour over chocolate and add cayenne, covering chocolate.

3. Let sit for 1–2 minutes.

4. Stir until chocolate is melted and all ingredients are fully incorporated.

PEANUT BUTTER WHIPPED CREAM:

1. Add the heavy cream, powdered sugar, and peanut butter into bowl.

2. Beat with an electric mixer for 4–7 minutes, or until stiff peaks form.

3. Fill piping bag with mixture and pipe out accordingly.

CANDIED CHOCOLATE BACON:

1. Preheat oven to 350°F.

2. Place a wire rack on a baking sheet. Arrange the bacon on the wire rack and sprinkle with the black pepper.

3. Lightly pat the brown sugar and cinnamon sugar on top of the bacon to create a thin layer.

4. Transfer the baking sheet to the oven and bake for 30–35 minutes or until the brown sugar has melted and the bacon is crisp.

5. Remove from the oven and allow to cool for 10 minutes.

6. Pour bacon chili ganache over bacon strips, then drizzle with melted white chocolate.

7. Sprinkle crushed pistachios and almonds over the top.

Head Cook:
Jack MacMurray

Team Name:
Jack Mac

Smoked bacon and Hershey's chocolate-wrapped pork belly over smoked bacon jam over a smoked bacon and Hershey's chocolate pancake. Topped with Szechuan glaze with Hershey's chocolate and smoked bacon bits.

Cook Time: 40 Minutes | Makes 4–6 servings

Ingredients

SMOKED BACON JAM:

1 pound smoked bacon, ¼" sliced

2 cups diced yellow onion

1 cup light brown sugar

2 ounces bourbon

4 ounces liquid coffee

1 tablespoon balsamic vinegar

SZECHUAN GLAZE:

½ cup minced ginger

½ cup minced garlic

2 cups Thai sweet chili sauce

2 cups honey

1½ cups light brown sugar

2 cups soy sauce

2 cups hoisin

Zest and juice of 1 lemon

Zest and juice of 1 orange

Zest and juice of 1 lime

2 cups cubed pineapple

1 teaspoon red pepper flakes

¼ cup freshly chopped basil

¼ cup chopped cilantro

¼ cup chopped green onions

¼ cup sriracha

¼ cup hot sauce (I used Cholula)

1 teaspoon sesame oil

1 tablespoon sesame seeds, toasted

½ cup chocolate chips (I used Hershey's)

PANCAKES:

2 cups pancake mix

1 cup buttermilk

1 cup bacon bits

1 cup chocolate chips (I used Hershey's)

BACON WRAPPED PORK BELLY:

12 slices smoked bacon

1 cup chocolate chips, to taste (I used Hershey's)

6 cups pork stock

12 ounces pork belly, cooked and cubed into 1½" chunks (11 total)

Directions

SMOKED BACON JAM:

1. In a saucepan, cook cut bacon for 5–6 minutes.

2. Add diced onions and cook until soft.

3. Add bourbon, then add brown sugar and coffee. Simmer 6–7 minutes until thickened.

4. Finish with balsamic vinegar.

SZECHUAN GLAZE:

1. In a saucepan, add ginger, garlic, Thai sauce, honey, brown sugar, soy sauce, hoisin, pineapple, red pepper flakes, basil, cilantro, green onions, sriracha, hot sauce, sesame oil, sesame seeds, and zest and juice from lemon, lime, and orange.

2. Bring to a boil then lower to a simmer. Cook 10–12 minutes.

3. Purée with an immersion blender.

4. Return to heat and whisk in chocolate to taste. Reserve.

PANCAKES:

1. In a mixing bowl whisk pancake mix, buttermilk, bacon bits, and chocolate chips to desired wetness.

2. In large nonstick sauté pan, make 11 pancakes. Set aside.

BACON WRAPPED PORK BELLY:

1. Cook smoked bacon for 14 minutes.

2. Melt chocolate chips.

3. Heat pork stock.

4. Smear melted chocolate onto bacon slices. Place cubed pork belly on each slice and roll up.

ASSEMBLY:

1. Place pancake down, then top with bacon jam.

2. Place bacon-wrapped pork belly on top.

3. Top with Szechuan glaze and chocolate.

4. Garnish with bacon bits.

"People who love to eat are always the best people."

—Julia Child

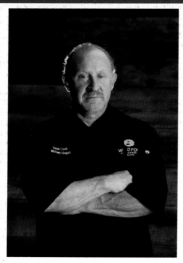

Head Cook:
Michael Hogan

Team Name:
Chef Michael Hogan
Omaha, NE

Business Name:
Spice Your Life Rub
Your Meats Foods

Facebook:
Spice Your Life Rub
Your Meat BBQ

Instagram:
@SpiceYourLifeRubYourMeat

www.SpiceYourLifeRubYourMeats.com

Indulge your taste buds with this incredible Bacon Bliss Pizza Pie that starts with a crust made from Greek yogurt and self-rising flour. Toasted crust is lightly brushed with extra virgin olive oil and gently sprinkled with pecorino Romano cheese. Bacon is layered on a bold tomato sauce with a Sicilian touch and fresh sliced mozzarella cheese. Topped with a crumble of chopped bacon, chopped sundries tomatoes, and chiffonade basil. The pizza is finished with a drizzle of aged balsamic vinegar.

Cook Time: 1 Hour | Makes 4–6 servings

Ingredients

CRUST:

2 cups self-rising flour

1 cup Greek yogurt

SAUCE:

¼ cup extra virgin olive oil

2 tablespoons Sicilian spice blend (I used Mie Radici)

1 tablespoon Greek oregano

1 28-ounce can crushed tomatoes

1 teaspoon salt

2 teaspoons sugar

4–5 sundried tomatoes, diced

CANDIED BACON:

2 pounds sliced bacon

1 tablespoon BBQ rub (I used Three Little Pigs Touch of Cherry Rub)

1 cup turbinado sugar

¼ teaspoon baking soda

1 tablespoon brown sugar

ADDITIONAL PIZZA INGREDIENTS:

4 tablespoons aged balsamic

8–10 leaves fresh basil

½ pound fresh mozzarella

Pecorino cheese

Sundried tomatoes

Directions

CRUST:

1. Combine yogurt and self-rising flour.
2. Knead until smooth and allow to rest for 20 minutes.

SAUCE:

1. In medium saucepan, over low to medium heat, add two tablespoons olive oil and combine herb blends. Heat for about five minutes until flavors are infused.
2. Add one can of crushed tomatoes.
3. Increase to medium heat, then add sugar and salt.
4. Continue cooking until sauce is reduced by one third. Remove from heat.
5. Add diced sundried tomatoes to sauce, just prior to assembling on pizza.

CANDIED BACON:

1. Lay bacon on a parchment paper-lined baking sheet.
2. Mix BBQ rub, turbinado sugar, baking soda, and brown sugar.
3. Coat bacon with mixture.

4. Bake at 350°F until bacon is sticky and cooked.

PIZZA:

1. Spray grill with nonstick cooking spray.
2. Separate dough in half and roll out to a quarter of an inch.
3. Place raw dough on prepared grill and cook both sides until golden brown, about 2 minutes. Remove from grill and brush with olive oil.
4. Spread prepared pizza sauce evenly over crust and bacon.
5. Lay partially cooked bacon slices from side to side.
6. Dress with fresh mozzarella and pecorino cheese and sprinkle with Sicilian spice blend.
7. Place in oven at 425°F for about 5 minutes or until cheese begins to brown.
8. Remove from oven and dress with candied bacon, chiffonade fresh basil, and sundried tomatoes, then drizzle with aged balsamic.

"*Food is our common ground, a universal experience.*"

—James Beard

Bacon Confit Shrimp with Bourbon Beurre Blanc

Head Cook:
Jean-Paul Lavallee

Team Name:
Chef Jean-Paul The Bacon Whisperer
Gulfport, MS

> **TIP:**
> - You can substitute a cipollini onion with a pearl onion or shallot.

Shrimp confit in bacon fat wrapped in hickory bacon set atop bacon-infused risotto and finished with a bourbon beurre blanc.

Cook Time: 1 Hour, 30 Minutes | Makes 4–6 servings

Ingredients

BACON-WRAPPED SHRIMP:
Bacon fat
1 teaspoon blackened seasoning
Shrimp, 2 per serving
Bacon slices, 2 per serving

BACON RISOTTO:
⅓ cup butter
½ pound bacon, diced
4 cloves black garlic, minced
1 cipollini onion
1 cup Arborio rice
⅓ cup pork stock
⅓ cup white wine
⅓ cup heavy cream
¼ cup aged Gouda cheese
Chives, chopped, to taste

BOURBON BEURRE BLANC:
⅓ cup bourbon
Juice of ½ lemon
⅓ cup heavy cream
¼ cup butter
Thyme sprig
Salt, to taste
Pepper, taste

GARNISH:
White asparagus
⅓ cup sushi vinegar
Hickory almonds

Directions

BACON-WRAPPED SHRIMP:
1. Preheat oven to 300°F.
2. Peel and clean shrimp.
3. Cover shrimp completely in bacon fat and place in oven for 5 minutes.
4. Lightly season shrimp and wrap in bacon strips.
5. Sear wrapped shrimp in a hot cast-iron pan.

BACON RISOTTO:
1. Melt butter in pan. Add cipollini and sauté until tender.
2. Add diced bacon. Cook until browned.
3. Add Arborio rice and lightly toast.
4. Slowly add pork stock and white wine until all is reduced.
5. Add heavy cream and cook down.
6. Fold in Gouda cheese.
7. Finish risotto with minced black garlic and chives.

BOURBON BEURRE BLANC:
1. Reduce bourbon, lemon juice, thyme, and cipollini.
2. Add heavy cream and bring to light boil.
3. Finish with butter, salt, and pepper.

GARNISH:
1. Use a vegetable peeler to ribbon out white asparagus. Soak in ice with sushi vinegar.
2. Toast almonds and lightly chop.

ASSEMBLY:
1. Add risotto to plate.
2. Top risotto with two shrimp.
3. Finish with beurre blanc.
4. Garnish with white asparagus and toasted almonds.

"Cooking is multisensory. It's made for the eyes, the mouth, the nose, the ear, and the soul. No other art is as complex."

—Pierre Gagnaire

Pinakbet is a Filipino traditional dish from the northern regions of the Philippines. It is usually made with pork and a mixture of vegetables, such as eggplant, okra, long beans, kabocha, and fish sauce or shrimp paste. It is served with rice. I enjoy cooking this dish whenever it comes up because it brings back memories of my childhood when my mother used to cook it. The wonderful aromas that permeate the kitchen overwhelm you, and you just want to eat it before it's done. When enjoyed with either friends or family, the love you put into this dish really comes out, and you can feel it.

Prep & Cook Time: 45 Minutes–1 Hour | Makes 4–6 servings

Head Cook:
Jayson Malla

Team Name:
OG808
San Francisco, CA

Instagram:
@SHAKA_SPOON_FORK

Ingredients

BACON GARLIC FRIED RICE:

2 cups medium grain rice

1 tablespoon + 1 teaspoon minced garlic

½ cup cooked bacon, chopped

½ cup thinly sliced green onions

Pinch kosher salt

Pinch black pepper

BACON PINAKBET:

14 ounces bacon, diagonally chopped

¾ cup diced onions

¾ cup chopped long beans

1½ cups diced kabocha squash

¾ cup round-cut okra

1 cup quartered eggplant

1 tablespoon finely chopped garlic

1 tablespoon finely chopped ginger

2 tablespoons sliced green onion

2 14.5-ounce cans diced tomatoes (I used Red Gold Petite Diced Tomatoes with Green Chilies)

4 tablespoons fish sauce

SHOYU DASHI EGG:

6 whole eggs

6 tablespoons soy sauce

1 bag dashi mix

Directions

BACON GARLIC FRIED RICE:

1. In a medium pot, add rice and wash and rinse until water is clear. Then fill it up with water (1:1 ratio), bring to a boil, and let simmer until done. Keep warm until needed.

2. Heat a large sauté pan to medium-high heat, then add chopped bacon and cook and render fat.

3. Remove cooked bacon and save for later. Use the bacon fat to cook the garlic until golden brown, then add cooked rice and fry for about 5 minutes.

4. Add the cooked bacon to the rice and toss until combined. Season with salt and pepper, then garnish with sliced green onions.

BACON PINAKBET:

1. Bring a large pot to medium-high heat and add olive oil.

2. Add bacon and cook to render fat. Cook until golden brown. Remove the bacon to save for later and leave drippings in the pot.

3. Add onions, garlic, ginger, and cook until aromatic and onions are translucent. Add diced petite tomatoes with green chiles and cook for about 5 minutes. With a hand blender, purée mixture until smooth and let simmer. Add the other diced petite tomatoes with green chiles and bring to boil once more.

4. Add fish sauce and let simmer. Then add squash and cook for 3 minutes. Then add okra and long beans and cook until tender but still crisp. Add the cooked bacon back with all the vegetables.

SHOYU DASHI EGG:

1. Fill a small pot with water and bring to a boil. Once boiling, drop in whole eggs and cook for about 6–8 minutes.

2. While eggs are cooking, fill another pot with 1½ cup warm water. Add soy sauce and dashi packet and set aside.

3. Once eggs are cooked, shock eggs in an ice bath. When the eggs are cool, peel the eggs and transfer to soy dashi mixture and let eggs sit until needed.

"The secret ingredient to good cooking is,
first, having a love of it."

—Jayson Malla

Bacon Roll Surf'N'Turf

Head Cook:
Jon Dye

Team Name:
Waynesville Career Center
Culinary Arts
Waynesville, MO

Slow roasted, chili seasoned hickory smoked bacon, rolled and seared, served over a bacon crusted seared scallop on a bed of asparagus and cremini mushrooms with a bacon whisky barbeque sauce, topped with Gouda cheese and microgreen garnish.

Cook Time: 45 Minutes | Makes 4–6 servings

Ingredients

CHILI RUB:

4 tablespoons paprika

4 tablespoons brown sugar

3 tablespoons salt

3 tablespoons garlic powder

1 tablespoon black pepper

1 tablespoon chili powder

1 tablespoon onion powder

2 tablespoons chipotle chili powder

1½ teaspoons cayenne pepper

1½ teaspoons cumin

1½ teaspoons dry mustard

WHISKY BARBECUE SAUCE:

½ pound bacon

½ cup whisky (I used Crown Royal)

2¾ cup ketchup

½ cup yellow mustard

¼ cup apple cider vinegar

¾ cup brown sugar

4 teaspoons chili powder

½ teaspoon cayenne pepper

¾ cup Worcestershire sauce

½ cup liquid smoke

½ teaspoon onion powder

½ teaspoon garlic powder

ASPARAGUS AND CREMINI MUSHROOMS:

4 cups water, salted

2 pounds asparagus ends (1½–2" long)

1 pound cremini mushrooms, quartered

3 garlic cloves, minced

1½ shallots, minced

BACON:

15 slices bacon

8 ounces butter

SCALLOPS:

⅓ pound bacon

13 scallops

3 tablespoons olive oil

1 tablespoon butter

GARNISH:

1 3-ounce wedge Gouda cheese

1 package microgreens

TIP:

- Cremini mushrooms are a different name for baby portobello mushrooms.

Directions

CHILI RUB:

1. In a bowl, combine paprika, brown sugar, salt, garlic powder, black pepper, chili powder, onion powder, chipotle chili powder, cayenne pepper, cumin, and dry mustard.
2. Mix and set aside.

WHISKY BARBECUE SAUCE:

1. Dice bacon and add to a saucepan.
2. Add ketchup, yellow mustard, apple cider vinegar, brown sugar, chili powder, cayenne pepper, Worcestershire sauce, liquid smoke, onion powder, and garlic powder and simmer for 30 minutes.
3. Remove sauce from heat and run through mesh strainer into sauce bottle.

ASPARAGUS AND CREMINI MUSHROOMS:

1. In a stock pot, simmer salted water.
2. Blanch asparagus tips and set aside.
3. Combine asparagus with quartered mushrooms in a skillet.
4. Lightly season with chili rub and sauté.
5. Add shallot and garlic.
6. When done, remove asparagus and mushrooms from the pan and set aside.
7. Deglaze the pan with whisky. Reduce slightly and add reduced mixture to BBQ sauce.

BACON:

1. On a sheet pan, sprinkle 15 slices of bacon with the chili rub.
2. Cook the bacon, flipping once. Bacon should be cooked through, but still pale.
3. Roll the bacon and secure with a toothpick.
4. Heat bacon fat and butter in a pan. Sear the rolled bacon in the mixture until a deep mahogany color. Then, place in the oven with a drip pan.

SCALLOPS:

1. In a sauté pan, brown bacon until just crisp.
2. Mince to powder, pat dry with paper towels, and set aside.
3. Season dried scallops with salt and pepper.
4. Heat olive oil and butter in a sauté pan.
5. Sear scallops.
6. Immediately after searing, dip the edge of the scallop in the BBQ sauce lightly.
7. Roll the sauced edge through fine bacon powder to crust.

ASSEMBLY:

1. Add sauce to the plate.
2. Make a bed of asparagus and mushrooms.
3. Rest the scallop on top.
4. Remove toothpick from rolled bacon. Add rolled bacon on top.
5. Garnish with shaved Gouda and microgreens.

"Taste as you go. When you taste the food throughout the cooking process, you can make adjustments as you go."

—Anne Burrell

Head Cook:
Jodi Taffel

Team Name:
The Fabulous Bacon Babe
Monrovia, CA

Business Name:
Bacon Babe Catering

Facebook:
Jodi Taffel; Bacon Babe Catering

Instagram:
@The.Bacon.Babe

This is a Blackberry Ginger Balsamic Braised Bacon "Steak" on top of a sweet corn and jalapeño nage with ginger scallion relish and handmade bacon caviar. I can't really describe my inspiration behind any dish, to be frank, because I never know when inspiration will hit. Sometimes I'm inspired by a particular ingredient. Sometimes I'm inspired by something I see on television or in a restaurant. Sometimes it's as simple as finding a plate that I really like and want to use.

Cook Time: 1 Hour | Makes 4–6 servings

Ingredients

BACON STEAK:

4 pounds slab bacon

2 cups blackberry ginger balsamic vinegar

½ cup apple cider vinegar

½ cup blueberries

6 cloves garlic

4 tablespoons tarragon

2 tablespoons tomato sauce (I used Red Gold Chili Ready)

2 tablespoons BBQ sauce (I used John Boy & Billy's Sweet & Mild)

2 tablespoons black peppercorns

2 teaspoons paprika

SWEET CORN & JALAPEÑO NAGE:

4 ears of corn

1 pint heavy cream

2 shallots

1 ounce red wine vinegar

2 ounces white wine

1 bay leaf

⅓ of a jalapeño pepper

1 teaspoon salt

GINGER SCALLION RELISH:

¼ cup ginger paste

¼ cup grapeseed oil

1 teaspoon soy sauce

1 teaspoon red wine vinegar

1½ teaspoons sesame oil

¼ teaspoon salt

1 cup scallions

1 teaspoon sesame seeds for garnish

BACON CAVIAR:

4 cups grapeseed oil

2 tablespoons bacon base

1 cup water

2 tablespoons agar-agar

10 drops red food coloring

1 pint blackberries, for garnish

Pinch of bacon salt

Directions

BACON STEAK:

1. Slice bacon into 12 equal-sized pieces and place in a heavy-bottomed pot or Dutch oven.
2. Add remaining ingredients into a blender and blend until everything is broken down.
3. Pour contents of blender over bacon, cover with a tight-fitting lid, and set over medium-low heat.
4. Braise bacon for 60 minutes.

SWEET CORN & JALAPEÑO NAGE:

1. Place corn in boiling water and cook for 10 minutes.
2. Transfer corn to a cutting board and remove kernels from cobs.
3. Blend corn and ¼ cup heavy cream in a blender until smooth.
4. Slice shallots and add to a saucepan over medium heat with the red wine vinegar, white wine, and bay leaf. Cook until reduced by about ¾.
5. Add the cream to the reduction and bring to a slow boil. Let the cream continue to boil and reduce until lightly thickened.
6. While the cream is reducing, remove the seeds from the jalapeño and finely dice.
7. Add the corn and jalapeño to the cream and continue to reduce until thick enough to coat the back of a spoon.
8. Salt to taste.

GINGER SCALLION RELISH:

1. Mix everything except sesame seeds together in a bowl and set aside.

BACON CAVIAR:

1. Pour one cup grapeseed oil into each of 4 bowls set over ice.
2. Whisk bacon base and food coloring into water and boil.
3. Add agar-agar and let melt into boiling liquid for 1 minute.
4. Pour liquid into the bottom of a caviar maker and cover with pipette tray.
5. Draw liquid up into the droppers and slowly drop balls into one bowl of grapeseed oil.
6. Repeat the last step 3 more times using the remaining bowls.
7. Remove bacon caviar from the oil and drop in cold water.
8. Cut blackberries into thick slices.

ASSEMBLY:

1. Ladle 1 heaping spoonful of corn nage onto the plate.
2. Carefully place one bacon "steak" on top of the nage.
3. Top each "steak" with a quenelle of ginger scallion relish, some sesame seeds, and a sprinkling of bacon caviar.
4. Place sliced blackberries in the corner of each plate and top with a pinch of bacon salt and more bacon caviar.

*"I love cooking with wine.
Sometimes I even put it in the food."*
—Julia Child

This is my version of steak, bacon, and potato ranchero. It's a bacon-wrapped cube stuffed full of seasoned bacon, steak, chopped fried potatoes, shredded Mexican cheese blend, and a slice of fried, crispy, salted pork belly. Served with a creamy tomato chipotle and garlic cilantro lime sour cream sauce and topped with a sweet heat salsa. Garnish with fresh cilantro and a lime wedge.

Cook Time: 45 Minutes | Makes 4–6 servings

Head Cook:
Jennifer Norem

Team Name:
Chef Jen & Team Indiana

Instagram:
@ChefJenNorem_74

Ingredients

2 pounds bacon, diced (I used Indiana Kitchen)

2 pounds New York strip steak, thinly chopped

1 16-ounce package four-cheese Mexican blend

2 pounds salted pork belly

½ cup peanut oil

MARINADE FOR STEAK:

1 teaspoon ranchero marinade (I used Grill Mates Smoky Ranchero)

1 packet coriander and annatto seasoning (I used Goya's Sazón with Coriander & Annatto)

2 tablespoons garlic powder

2 tablespoons chili lime seasoning

1 teaspoon smoked paprika

1 teaspoon hickory smoke powder

½ cup lime juice

½ tablespoon kosher salt

DRY MIXTURE FOR DICED POTATOES:

5 large red potatoes, diced

⅓ cups olive oil

2 teaspoons chili lime seasoning

2 tablespoons ranchero marinade (I used Grill Mates Smoky Ranchero)

TOMATO CHIPOTLE LIME SOUR CREAM SAUCE:

1 16-ounce package sour cream

½ teaspoon chipotle seasoning

½ can petite diced tomatoes with green chilies, lightly puréed, (I used Red Gold)

3 limes, juiced

LIME GARLIC CILANTRO CREAM SAUCE:

4 cloves garlic, finely minced

2 cups sour cream

1 large lime, juiced

½ bunch fresh cilantro, finely chopped

1 teaspoon kosher salt

½ teaspoon cracked pepper

SWEET HEAT SALSA:

1 14.5-ounce can petite diced tomatoes with green chilies (I used Red Gold)

⅛ cup tomato sauce (I used Red Gold)

1 bunch fresh cilantro, chopped

2 cloves garlic, minced

⅓ cup chopped white onion

2 large limes, juiced

2 tablespoons sugar

1 teaspoon salt

2 tablespoons pico de gallo seasoning (I used Bolner Fiesta)

BACON WRAP:

3 pounds bacon, thinly sliced (I used Indiana Kitchen Bacon)

GARNISH:

Cilantro sprigs

Lime slices

Hot sauce

Directions

1. Prepare steak:
2. Cut ½" long, thin slices, about ⅛" thick. In a non-corrosive bowl, add steak and all ingredients for marinade, mix well, and let sit while preparing other ingredients.
3. Prepare the diced potatoes:
4. Cut potatoes into small bite-sized cubes and rinse. Drain well. In a bowl, combine potatoes, all dry ingredients, and olive oil. Cover and set aside.
5. Prepare tomato chipotle sauce:
6. In mixing bowl, add all ingredients and mix well, until fully blended. This can be done with a hand whisk.
7. In a mini food processor, combine all ingredients for lime garlic cilantro sauce and process for 1 minute or until ingredients are finely processed. In a mixing bowl add 2 cups sour cream and fold in ingredients to fully incorporate. Do not add sour cream to food processor, as this will become soupy.
8. In another bowl, add all ingredients for salsa and gently mix. Set aside.
9. In a large skillet or cast iron pan over medium heat, add the diced bacon and chopped steak. Cook until both meats are fully cooked. Remove from heat and drain excess fat.
10. Cut salted pork belly into 2" lengths. In a cast iron pan on low to medium heat, fry salted pork belly until lightly browned and crispy.
11. In a 12-inch cast iron pan, add ¼ cup peanut oil to cover diced potatoes for frying. Oil temperature should be 375°F–380°F. Cook potatoes until golden brown, remove

> *"Cooking is a philosophy; it's not a recipe."*
> —Marco Pierre White

DIRECTIONS CONTINUED

from oil, and place on paper towels to remove excess oil.

12. In a large mixing bowl, combine the cooked bacon, steak, potatoes, and shredded cheese. Mix until incorporated.

13. Prepare the bacon for wrapping by cutting bacon in equal halves. Place 2 slices of bacon next to each other horizontally and then two slices over vertically to form a cross. In middle of bacon, add 1 piece of salted pork belly. Then add 2–3 tablespoons meat and potato mixture on top of pork belly. Fold over vertical bacon and then horizontal bacon to completely cover mixture. Then mold bacon to create a cube. Add toothpicks to hold bacon ends together and place on 11x16 cookie sheet about 2" apart.

14. Bake in oven on 380°F for 20 minutes and then on broil for 10 minutes to crisp bacon.

15. On a plate, add 2 tablespoons tomato chipotle cream to one side of the plate and then 2 tablespoons lime cilantro sauce on opposite side of plate. Place bacon-wrapped ranchero in middle and top with 1 to 1½ tablespoons salsa.

16. Side garnish with cilantro and lime wedge and few drops hot sauce. Serve and enjoy.

Head Cook:
Rebecka Evans

Team Name:
At Home with Rebecka
Castle Rock, CO

Facebook:
At Home with Rebecka

Instagram:
@AtHomeWithRebecka

www.AtHomeWithRebecka.com

My BLT Cupcake (aka bacon, lemon, and tomato cupcake) may sound like a savory dish, but it's a perfectly sweet dessert capturing every aspect of cupcake texture and taste with the umami of bacon.

The recipe starts with a vanilla crumb cake laced with tomatoes and green chilies, a hint of lemon zest, and sugared bacon dust. The cake is topped with a sweet tomato bacon jam, and then frosted with a swirl of vanilla and tomato butter cream, dressed in a bacon swizzle drizzled with white chocolate. Surprisingly, the tomatoes take on a rich lemony flavor, adding a delightful depth of flavor to the cupcakes.

Inspiration for the recipe comes from on one of my favorite heirloom recipes, Condensed Tomato Soup Cake, that was made popular in the 1930s when the soup took the place of milk and dairy products, adding moisture and texture. This decadent cupcake finished 7th in the Word Food Championships Bacon Top Ten Round 2018 and was the first bacon cupcake ever submitted in the category; a truly decadent bacon-infused dessert.

Cook Time: 15–20 Minutes | Makes 12–16 cupcakes

Ingredients

CUPCAKES:

1 cup cooked bacon (I used Indiana Kitchen)

1¼ cups cake flour

2 teaspoons baking powder

½ teaspoon salt

¼ cup bacon grease, cooled

2 tablespoons butter, room temperature

1 cup sugar

Grated zest 1 large lemon

⅓ cup sour cream (Note: do not use low fat)

1 teaspoon vanilla

3 egg whites, room temperature

¼ cup whole milk

1 tablespoon diced tomato pulp (I used Red Gold Tomatoes with Green Chilies)

¼ cup diced tomato liquid (I used Red Gold Tomatoes with Green Chilies)

¼ cup sugared bacon dust (recipe below)

CANDY BACON:

1 cup cooked bacon (I used Indiana Kitchen)

1 cup light brown sugar

1 teaspoon fresh ground black pepper

SWEET TOMATO BACON JAM:

¼ pound thick cut bacon (I used Indiana Kitchen)

2 teaspoons fresh lemon juice

1 teaspoon pepper

1 teaspoon sea salt with red pepper flakes

2 tablespoon tomato paste (I used Red Gold)

2 tablespoons diced tomatoes (I used Red Gold Tomatoes with Green Chilies)

1 tablespoon water, if needed to thin

¼ cup light brown sugar

SUGARED BACON DUST:

½ cup cooked bacon, chopped (I used Indiana Kitchen)

1½ teaspoon granulated sugar

BACON SWIZZLE STICKS:

8 paper towel sections

8 slices center cut thin cut bacon (I used Indiana Kitchen)

8 discs white melting chocolate

BACON TOMATO FROSTING:

1 cup (2 sticks) butter cut into chunks (must be cold)

2 tablespoons cooled bacon fat

3 cups powder sugar (plus ¼ cup for color if needed)

2 teaspoon vanilla

½ teaspoon salt

4–6 tablespoons heavy whipping cream

1 tablespoon tomato paste (I used Red Gold)

4 squirts red food gel

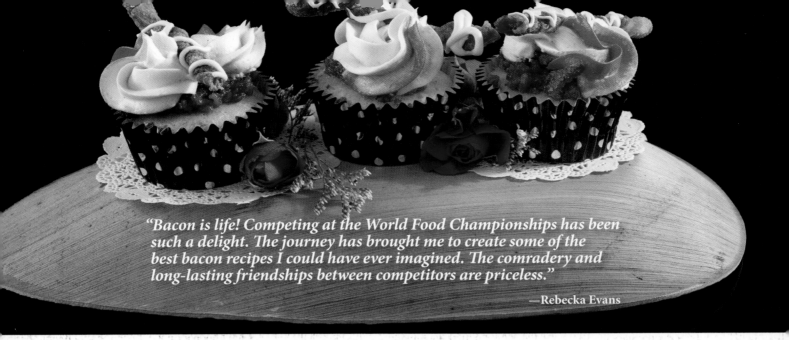

"Bacon is life! Competing at the World Food Championships has been such a delight. The journey has brought me to create some of the best bacon recipes I could have ever imagined. The comradery and long-lasting friendships between competitors are priceless."

—Rebecka Evans

Directions

CUPCAKES:

1. Preheat the oven to 350°F.
2. Line muffin cups with cupcake liners.
3. Cook chopped bacon in a large pan until crisp, drain on paper towel, and reserve bacon fat.
4. Make sugared bacon dust (recipe below).
5. Sift the flour, baking powder, and salt in a bowl—set aside.
6. In a stand mixer, blend bacon grease, butter, and sugar together until blended.
7. Add lemon zest, sour cream, and vanilla.
8. Mix until combined.
9. Add the egg whites and beat well, scraping down the bowl often. Don't over mix.
10. Add the flour mixture to the batter in 3 batches, alternating with the milk and tomatoes.
11. Beat on low speed for a minute, scraping down the sides to ensure all the ingredients are incorporated into the batter. The batter will be loose/wet.
12. Fold ¼ cup sugared bacon dust into batter.
13. Fill the cupcake liners ½ full with batter (do not overfill). Makes 12–16 cupcakes.
14. Bake for 15–18 minutes, or until a toothpick inserted in the center comes out clean. Do not overcook.
15. Remove the cupcakes from the oven and let cool 5 minutes before removing from the pan.
16. Cool cupcakes completely before frosting.
17. Spread bacon jam over the cooled cupcakes leaving just a small rim of cake untouched by jam.
18. Sprinkle with candy bacon over jam.
19. Frost and garnish with bacon swizzle stick (recipe below).

CANDY BACON:

1. Chop bacon and cook until almost crisp.
2. Add brown sugar and pepper. Stir to combine.
3. Cook 3–5 minutes stirring constantly. Remove from pan and cool on a piece of parchment.
4. Chop into bits.

SWEET TOMATO BACON JAM:

1. Cut bacon slices into thirds. Divide pepper into thirds. Pepper each batch of bacon and cook in batches until crisp.
2. Add sea salt with pepper flakes to last batch of bacon.
3. Remove all but 2 tablespoons bacon fat from pan. Add tomatoes, lemon juice, tomato paste, and brown sugar and cook until thick, about 3–5 minutes.
4. Add 1 tablespoon water if the mixture is too thick.
5. Pour mixture into a small food processor. Add cooked bacon and blend until mixture is very fine. Cool.
6. Spread jam over top of cupcake before adding candy bacon bits.

SUGARED BACON DUST:

1. Place bacon and sugar in a spice grinder and pulverize.

BACON SWIZZLE STICKS:

1. Twist bacon strips one at a time until very tightly twisted. Lay bacon twist on a piece of paper towel and roll the bacon up in the towel.
2. Continue until all bacon is twisted and wrapped in paper towel.
3. Place all 8 rolled twists in a microwave oven.
4. Cook 6 minutes. Check for doneness and rotate outer pieces into the middle for even cooking. Cook additional 3 minutes until bacon is just done.
5. Unwrap immediately and keep at room temp on a cooling rack.
6. Once bacon twists are cooled, break each in half.
7. Melt white chocolate in microwave for 30 seconds. Stir to blend. Cook additional 15–30 seconds as needed.
8. Drizzle over bacon twists.
9. Keep sticks on a towel until ready to plate.

BACON TOMATO FROSTING:

1. Beat cold butter, cooled bacon fat, powdered sugar, and salt in a mixer until smooth and creamy.
2. Add vanilla.
3. Start adding heavy cream 1 tablespoon at a time until desired consistency.
4. Remove ¾ of the white frosting to a medium piping bag. Snip off the end to create a medium-sized opening for easy piping.
5. Add 1 tablespoon tomato paste to remaining frosting and blend until combined, scraping down the edges of the mixer often. (To create deeper red color, add red coloring. I used 4 squirts red gel food coloring. Blend until smooth.)
6. Add ¼ cup powdered sugar to tighten frosting.
7. Fill a small piping bag with red coloring. Snip a tiny hole in the bottom of the bag. Pipe a thin strip of red frosting into a larger piping bag fitted with a medium "open flower" tip. Fill the bag by piping in the white frosting.
8. Make a few test swirls until frosting comes out multi-colored.

Bombay BLT

Head Cook:
Daniel Carberg

Team Name:
Carby Carberg
Roxbury, NH

Instagram:
@DCarberg

This is an Indian-inspired version of the classic BLT, featuring a biscuit made with bacon, a touch of garam masala, and black sesame seeds. Add a curried yogurt-mayo, Indian-spiced crispy baked bacon, a bacon-onion-tamarind chutney, a curried fried-green tomato (fried in bacon fat and ghee), and lemon-dressed watercress for a delicious Bombay BLT.

Prep & Cook Time: 1 Hour, 15 Minutes | Makes 6 servings

Ingredients

- 5 cups all-purpose flour
- 6 tablespoons sugar
- 2 teaspoons salt
- 4 teaspoons baking powder
- ½ teaspoon cream of tartar
- 1½ sticks unsalted butter
- 4 eggs
- 1 cup whole milk
- 3 10-ounce packages hickory smoked bacon (I used Pederson's)
- 2 tablespoons black sesame seeds

- 3 tablespoons garam masala
- 6 tablespoons ghee
- 2 teaspoons turmeric
- 2 teaspoons ground ginger
- 2 teaspoons paprika
- ½ teaspoon cayenne pepper
- 2 tablespoons black pepper
- 4 cups panko breadcrumbs
- 3 cups yellow cornmeal
- 1¼ cups mayo

- 4 tablespoons yellow curry powder
- 1½ cups plain Greek yogurt
- 1 large yellow onion, chopped
- 2 tablespoons tamarind pulp
- 1 tablespoon Dijon mustard
- 1½ tablespoons apple cider vinegar
- 4 green tomatoes
- 1 lemon
- 1 bunch watercress
- Salt and pepper, to taste

Directions

1. Preheat oven to 450°F.

2. Pan fry one package and a half of hickory smoked bacon in two different pans. When done, place bacon on paper towels to drain.

3. Grate butter and place in cooler.

4. In a bowl, combine 3 cups flour, 3 tablespoons sugar, ½ teaspoon salt, ½ teaspoon cream of tartar, and 1 teaspoon garam masala.

5. Finely chop 8 slices of the cooked bacon and set aside.

6. Combine the butter into the flour mixture, and then add the chopped bacon and 2 tablespoons of black sesame seeds.

7. Lightly roll out the dough and cut into 12 individual biscuits. Place on baking tray and bake for 15 minutes. When done, brush with 2 tablespoons melted ghee. Set aside on cooling rack and reduce heat of oven to 380°F.

8. Combine spices in bowl: 3 tablespoons garam masala, 2 teaspoons turmeric, 2 teaspoons ginger, 2 teaspoons paprika,

½ teaspoon cayenne pepper, 1 tablespoon sugar, and 1 tablespoon black pepper.

9. Press the spices into 12 slices of uncooked bacon and bake on a rack for approximately 15–20 minutes, flipping at least once. Remove when done and set aside.

10. While the bacon is cooking, take the remaining skillet-cooked bacon and chop it into pieces. Place them in a skillet and add one chopped onion, 1 tablespoon Dijon mustard, 1½ tablespoons apple cider vinegar, 2 tablespoons tamarind pulp, 1 teaspoon sugar, salt and pepper to taste, and ¼ cup water. Heat on medium. Once onions have begun to get tender, lower the heat to low, cover, and let simmer for 30 minutes. Add more liquid if it needs it. Once done, remove from heat and take off lid to let cool.

11. Slice tomatoes into 12 thin slices and start your dredging station. Station 1: 2 cups flour seasoned with salt and pepper. Station 2: 3 eggs and 2 tablespoons mayo, beaten. Station 3:

4 cups panko breadcrumbs, 3 cups yellow cornmeal, and 2 tablespoons yellow curry powder. Dredge slices in station 1, dip in the egg mixture in station 2, and then coat with the dry mixture in station 3.

12. Pan fry in reserved bacon grease plus 4 tablespoons ghee, using 2 separate pans on medium high heat for 4 minutes, then flip for another 4 minutes. Sit on cooling rack.

13. Combine 1½ cups Greek yogurt, 1 cup mayo, 2 tablespoons curry powder, 1 tablespoon lemon juice, and salt and pepper to taste. Set aside.

14. Coat watercress with juice of half a lemon.

15. Assemble: Slice biscuits in half and set out the bottoms. Add a teaspoon of the curry yogurt, then a fried tomato, a tablespoon of chutney, baked spiced bacon, and watercress. Then, add another teaspoon of curry yogurt to the top half of each biscuit and place on top.

"*The home kitchen is a judgement-free zone, where we should feel free to take any risk imaginable, validate our triumphs, and learn from our imperfections.*"

—Daniel Carberg

Bourbon Maple Bacon Cupcake

Head Cook:
Jordan James

Team Name:
Cupcakes by Jordan James
Waukesha, WI

Business Name:
Cupcakes by Jordan James

Facebook:
Cupcakes by Jordan James

Instagram:
@Cupcakes_By_Jordan_James

www.CupcakesByJordanJames.com

A light, cinnamon maple cake dipped in bourbon and topped with a layer of bacon, cold-smoked bacon-infused cream cheese frosting, brown sugar peach compote, finely minced bacon and bacon crumble, and garnished with a decorative smoked tuile.

I introduced my Maple Bacon cupcake at the 2018 Trek Cyclocross World Cup, where one of the fun traditions of race spectating is to hand bacon to riders! I figured if anyone could appreciate a bacon cupcake, it would be this crowd. I was 13 at the time. I entered my cupcake into the 2022 Milwaukee Bacon Fest just to have some fun and get a little exposure. For this competition, I added bourbon to the cupcake base and hickory liquid smoke to the frosting to give it more body and flavor. I was completely shocked when they announced I won by unanimous decision. This win qualified me for the World Food Championship—Bacon Category.

My goal for WFC was to create the best version of my cupcake. Instead of liquid smoke, I go through the process of cold smoking the frosting with hickory chips. I also top the cupcake with a cold-smoked, bacon-infused tuile, which is one of my favorite elements of this dish. I add a peach compote to brighten the dish and bring some refreshing notes to an otherwise savory cupcake. I finish the dish with a bacon crumble and minced bacon so that it's the first thing you taste. To me, the balance of flavors and textures along with the elegant aesthetic make this cupcake special.

Cook Time: 1 Hour, 30 Minutes | Makes 8 standard cupcakes, or 20 mini cupcakes

Ingredients

BACON:
2 packages (20–24 strips) hickory smoked bacon

CUPCAKES:
3 cups all-purpose flour
1 cup unsalted butter
2 cups sugar
6 tablespoons maple syrup
4 eggs
1⅓ cup milk
2 teaspoons cinnamon
2 teaspoons vanilla extract
1½ teaspoons baking powder
1 teaspoon salt
½ cup bourbon (for dipping)

PEACH COMPOTE:
1 10-ounce package frozen peaches
2½ tablespoons brown sugar
1 teaspoon balsamic vinegar
Pinch of salt
Water (enough to cover bottom of medium pan)
⅛ teaspoon nutmeg
¼ teaspoon cinnamon

FROSTING:
4 cups powdered sugar
8 ounces cream cheese
½ cup butter
2 tablespoons maple syrup
3 tablespoons bacon oil
Hickory wood chips (for cold smoking)

TUILE:
1 heaping tablespoon all-purpose flour
⅓ cup water
2 tablespoons bacon oil
¼ teaspoon paprika
Pinch of salt
Pinch of granulated sugar
Hickory wood chips (for cold smoking)

BACON CRUMBLE:
2 tablespoons bacon, finely minced
1 tablespoon flour
1½ teaspoons brown sugar
⅜ teaspoon granulated sugar
¼ tablespoon unsalted butter, melted

Directions

BACON:
1. Preheat oven to 375°F.
2. Line 2 large cookie sheets with parchment paper.
3. Lay bacon flat on parchment paper. Do not overlap the bacon.
4. Cook bacon in oven for 15–20 minutes, until crispy.
5. Place bacon on paper towel, carefully press to dry.
6. Save the bacon oil. Set aside for frosting and tuile.

CUPCAKE BASE:
1. Preheat oven to 350°F and line cupcake pan with liners.
2. Beat butter and sugar in mixer until light and fluffy.
3. Add eggs one at a time.

"'One touch.' This helps me focus on efficiency and quality. One touch simply means to do it right the first time."

—Jordan James

DIRECTIONS CONTINUED

4. Add flour, salt, baking powder, and cinnamon in mixer. Mix on slow.

5. While mixing, add maple syrup, milk, and vanilla extract until fully combined.

6. Scoop batter into cupcake liners. Fill cupcake liner ¾ full with batter.

7. Bake minis for approximately 14 minutes. Bake standard size for approximately 23 minutes. Cupcakes are done when you gently press the top of cupcake and it bounces back.

8. Place cupcakes on cooling rack. Let sit until fully cooled.

FROSTING:

1. In separate bowl, beat butter and cream cheese together in stand mixer.

2. Add powdered sugar. Mix thoroughly.

3. Add maple syrup. Mix thoroughly.

4. Add bacon oil. Mix thoroughly.

5. Place frosting on platter under bowl and cold smoke with hickory chips for 13 minutes.

6. Place smoked frosting in fridge to cool and set.

PEACH COMPOTE:

1. Dice frozen peaches.

2. Cook peaches, water, brown sugar, nutmeg, cinnamon, and salt in a medium pot on medium high heat until peaches soften.

3. Stir in balsamic vinegar.

4. Place compote in fridge to cool.

BACON PIECES:

1. Cut 1" pieces of bacon for minis, or 2" pieces of bacon for standards, until you have enough to top cupcakes (1 per cupcake).

MINCED BACON:

1. Mince enough bacon to set aside 2 tablespoons for bacon crumble and ¼ cup to garnish cupcakes.

BACON CRUMBLE:

1. Combine minced bacon, flour, brown sugar, and granulated sugar.

2. Melt unsalted butter and pour little by little into bacon mixture, stirring with fork until crumbly. Add a little more butter if mixture is not crumbly.

3. Line cookie sheet with parchment paper. Spread crumble onto parchment paper.

4. Cook in oven at 375°F for 5 minutes.

5. Remove and let cool.

TUILE:

1. Mix flour, water, bacon oil, and paprika until evenly combined. To thin tuile mixture, add 1 tablespoon of water at a time until you reach desired consistency.

2. Pour about 3 tablespoons of mixture into nonstick pan over medium-high heat, evenly coating the bottom of the pan.

3. Cook until mixture is set and stops bubbling.

4. Take tuile out with tweezers and place on paper towel.

5. Immediately sprinkle salt and granulated sugar on tuile. Allow tuile to dry and cool.

6. Place bowl over tuile and cold smoke with hickory chips for 5 minutes.

ASSEMBLY:

1. Pour bourbon into a small bowl.

2. Dip the top of the cupcake base in bourbon. Hold for a quick 3 seconds.

3. Pipe a small dab of frosting on top of cupcake base to secure bacon.

4. Press a strip of bacon into frosting and level. Strips of bacon should be about 1" long for minis, 2" for standards.

5. Frost the top of bacon.

6. Add peach compote.

7. Sprinkle bacon crumble and finely minced bacon on top of the peach compote.

8. Break piece of smoked tuile and place on cupcake to garnish.

Chocolate Chicken Lollipop
with Bacon Pear Chocolate Chutney

Head Cook:
Peter Radjou

Team Name:
Radjou's
Roanoke, VA

A chicken lollipop marinated and wrapped with bacon, double-fried for crispiness, and dipped in spiced Hershey chocolate, served with a blend of spicy pear bacon chocolate chutney. Chef Radjou was inspired by his two daughters' love for chicken wings and bacon. His creativity influenced sweet and savory by adding chocolate to this recipe. The pear chutney was motivated by the juicy pears from his garden.

Prep Time: 45 Minutes | Cook Time: 45 Minutes | Makes 4–6 servings

Ingredients

CHICKEN LOLLIPOPS:

1 12-ounce bag chocolate chips (I used Hershey's)

6 whole chicken wings

1 pound packages bacon

Oil (for frying)

¼ cup soy sauce

½ teaspoon granulated garlic

½ teaspoon black pepper

½ teaspoon ground ginger

½ cup corn starch (enough to coat chicken)

¼ teaspoon cayenne pepper

¼ teaspoon Himalayan pink salt

BACON PEAR CHOCOLATE CHUTNEY:

¼ cup chocolate chips (I used Hershey's)

6 strips bacon

2 pears

½ dry habanero pepper

½ teaspoon cayenne pepper

½ teaspoon Himalayan pink salt

1 teaspoon sugar

Directions

CHICKEN LOLLIPOPS:

1. French the chicken wings into chicken lollipops. (A technique using a paring knife to bring all the skin and flesh to one side of the bone by slitting one side to the other to create a lollipop.)

2. Marinate chicken lollipops in soy sauce, granulated garlic, ground ginger, black pepper, and cornstarch.

3. Deep fry until the internal temp is 160°F.

4. Cool, wrap with bacon, and secure it with a toothpick.

5. Deep fry again, to cook bacon until the bacon is crispy.

6. Melt chocolate chips and add cayenne pepper Himalayan salt. Mix well, dip chicken wings in chocolate mixture and set aside.

BACON PEAR CHOCOLATE CHUTNEY:

1. Chop bacon and sauté until crispy. Drain and reserve fat.

2. Peel and grate pears.

3. Add 1 tablespoon of bacon fat in a pan and sauté pears and dry habanero until the pears are cooked.

4. Add sugar, cayenne pepper, and salt, and blend along with half of the crisped bacon.

5. Transfer the pear chutney to a bowl and add chocolate chips immediately to melt. (Microwave if needed.)

6. Before serving, add the reserved bacon to the chutney.

7. To serve, add chutney, place the chicken lollipops on top and garnish with microgreens and edible flowers.

"*My simple and unique recipes are fueled by the love of my family.*"

—Peter Radjou

This traditional chocolate chip bourbon cake takes on a modern twist with unexpected flavor combinations and is made entirely from scratch. Served with bacon pecan crunch, chocolate bacon twists, three homemade sauces, a dollop of mascarpone whipped cream, fresh raspberries, and bacon dust. This delicate but rich desert also incorporates Hershey's chocolate chips in three unique ways.

The cake is infused with semi-sweet chocolate chips. Chocolate bacon twists are dipped in melted semi-sweet chocolate and drizzled with white chocolate chips, creating a chocolatey-bacon topper for the cakes. The cake is finished with a drizzle of melted chocolate and fresh raspberries, the proverbial cherry on top, raising this traditional cake to the peak of high fashion.

Prep Time: 20 Minutes | Cook Time: 20–25 Minutes
Makes 12 mini-Bundt pans, or 1 10-cup Bundt pan

Head Cook:
Rebecka Evans

Team Name:
At Home with Rebecka
Castle Rock, CO

Facebook:
At Home with Rebecka

Instagram:
@AtHomeWithRebecka

www.AtHomeWithRebecka.com

Ingredients

BOURBON CAKE:

1 10-ounce package dried pitted dates (17 whole dates) chopped into ½" pieces

2 teaspoons baking soda

¾ cup boiling water

¼ cup bourbon

½ cup unsalted butter, softened

1 cup + 2 tablespoons granulated sugar

3 eggs

1¾ cup self-rising flour

¾ cups chocolate chips

2 tablespoons Crisco, melted

1 cup turbinado sugar, for dusting pans

CARAMEL SAUCE:

½ cup unsalted butter

2 cups brown sugar

2 cups heavy cream

3 tablespoons bourbon

1 tablespoon vanilla extract

BACON PECAN CRUNCH:

16 slices bacon, divided

1½ cups chopped honey roasted pecans

1 cup brown sugar

½ cup unsalted butter

RASPBERRY COULIS:

6 ounces fresh raspberries

12 ounces frozen raspberries

3 tablespoons granulated sweetener (I used Pyure Organic Granulated Sweetener)

2 tablespoon lemon juice

BOURBON CREAM:

1 tablespoon bourbon

2 cups heavy whipping cream

½ cup sugar, divided

1 teaspoon vanilla extract

5 jumbo eggs, at room temperature, separate yolks and whites

¼ cup granulated sweetener (I used Pyure Organic Granulated Sweetener)

1 tablespoon vanilla bean paste or extract

CHOCOLATE DRIZZLE AND CHOCOLATE-DIPPED BACON TWISTS:

1 package semi-sweet chocolate chips, melted (I used Hershey's)

½ package white chocolate chips, melted (I used Hershey's)

1 pound thin cut bacon

MASCARPONE WHIP:

2 cups heavy cream

3 tablespoons sugar

1 8-ounce tub mascarpone

1 teaspoon vanilla extract

GARNISH:

1 bunch fresh mint

Directions

BOURBON CAKE:

1. Heat oven to 375°F.

2. Place chopped dates in a non-reactive bowl with baking soda, bourbon, and boiling water. Allow to soak for 15–20 minutes until the dates are softened. Place the date mixture in a food processor for 2 minutes to form a paste. (Do this in batches.)

3. Using a stand mixer fitted with the paddle attachment, cream butter on medium speed for about 1 minute. Add granulated sugar and continue to cream for 3 minutes longer. Scrape down the sides of the bowl using a rubber spatula. Add eggs, one at a time, mixing in between to fully incorporate each egg. Scrape down the sides of the bowl. With the mixer running on low, add self-rising flour, about ½ cup at a time, and mix just until the flour is no longer visible.

4. Remove the bowl from the stand mixer. Add the date paste, chocolate chips, and gently fold in using a rubber spatula.

Our family's motto growing up... Lat, we love you!

—Rebecka Evans

DIRECTIONS CONTINUED

5. Grease mini-Bundt pans with melted Crisco. Sprinkle the turbinado sugar into the baking or Bundt pan and move the pan around until the sugar coats the bottom and all sides. Dump out excess sugar. Bake 35–45 minutes or until toothpick inserted in the middle comes away clean.

6. Remove from oven and cool at room temperature for 10 minutes. Flip out of pans and place on serving plate.

CARAMEL SAUCE:

1. Place butter in a heavy-bottom sauce pot over medium heat. Once melted, add brown sugar and continue to cook for about 8 minutes, stirring occasionally.

2. Add heavy cream and allow to cook for another 6–7 minutes, still stirring occasionally.

3. Remove pan from heat and stir in bourbon and vanilla. Pour into small bowl to cool.

BACON PECAN CRUNCH:

1. Line a jelly roll pan with aluminum foil.

2. Chop and cook 16 slices of thick bacon until crisp.

3. Add the chopped bacon and honey-roasted pecans to a lined baking sheet.

4. In a saucepan, mix brown sugar and butter together until the butter is melted and both ingredients are well combined stirring occasionally.

5. Allow to boil for about 3–4 minutes. Pour the mixture over the bacon evenly and stir to coat.

6. The toffee will harden as it cools; break apart into small chunks. Set aside until ready to build cake.

RASPBERRY COULIS:

1. Pour frozen raspberries and fresh raspberries into blender. Add sugars and lemon juice. Blend until smooth.

2. Place raspberry mix in a fine sieve fitted over a small mixing bowl.

3. Using a spatula, press as much juice out of raspberries as possible. Scrape the bottom of the sieve into the bowl. Scrape the bottom of the sieve again and discard the seeds.

BOURBON CREAM:

1. Bring heavy cream, ¼ cup sugar, and vanilla bean paste to simmer in a small- to medium-sized sauce pot.

2. In a mixing bowl, whisk the egg yolks and other ¼ cup sugar together until frothy.

3. While stirring, slowly add about ½ of the heavy cream mixture to the eggs. Stir together gently. Pour the egg mixture into the pot of remaining heavy cream. Continue to cook over medium-low heat until the mixture thickens and coats the back of a spatula or spoon, about 5–8 minutes.

4. Stir in the vanilla extract and bourbon and remove from heat. Pour the mixture through a strainer into a silicone measuring cup.

5. Place container of bourbon sauce in an ice bath until cool.

CHOCOLATE DRIZZLE AND CHOCOLATE-DIPPED BACON TWISTS:

1. Melt semi-sweet chocolate chips in microwave in 30-second intervals, stirring after each interval until chocolate is melted.

2. Melt white chocolate chips in microwave in 30-second intervals, stirring after each interval until melted.

3. Twist 12 strips thin cut bacon into long strips then wrap each twist tightly in individual paper towels.

4. Cook the bacon in 1-minute intervals in microwave, turning each interval. About 8 minutes for 12 pieces.

MASCARPONE WHIP:

1. Using a hand-held mixer, whip heavy cream, sugar, and mascarpone together in a large bowl until stiff peaks.

2. Add vanilla extract and blend.

3. Put whipped cream in pastry bag fitted with tip. Refrigerate.

ASSEMBLY:

1. Slice cooled cake.

2. Dress each piece with equal amounts of caramel sauce, bourbon cream, and raspberry coulis.

3. Top each with bacon crunch, dollop of mascarpone whipped cream, chocolate twist and melted chocolate drizzle, and fresh raspberries.

Head Cook:
Paula Todora

Team Name:
Paula Todora
Blue Eye, AR

This recipe is one of my favorites that came from my heart. Aren't they just adorable? And they're delicious, more than you can even imagine. I wish I was there with you to make a plateful for you. Even better, follow my easy directions to make a batch for yourself and your loved ones. Spread the love, baby!

Homemade bacon honey graham crackers shaped like little piggies are gussied up with minced cooked bacon and a little southern bacon grease and filled with a layer of handmade fluffy marshmallow cream that has been lightly toasted. Two slices of oven-cooked maple candied bacon are gently placed atop the marshmallow cream to give that sweet and salty taste we all desire. As if that isn't more than your taste buds can handle, before the second graham cracker is placed on top, rich chocolate ganache, made from Hershey's semi-sweet chocolate chips and rich whipping cream tops the bacon and drips down the sides.

Cook Time: 30 Minutes | Makes 12–20 s'mores

Ingredients

MAPLE CANDIED BACON:

½ pound hickory smoked bacon

¼ cup pure maple syrup

¼ cup light brown sugar

HOMEMADE BACON HONEY GRAHAM CRACKERS:

8 slices hickory smoked bacon, cut into 1" pieces

2 teaspoons bacon grease, cooled (reserved from cooking bacon)

1 cup unsalted butter, chilled and cut into 1" slices

1 cup dark brown sugar, packed

¼ cup honey

¼ cup whole milk

2 teaspoons pure vanilla extract

1 cup unbleached white flour

2 cups whole wheat flour

½ teaspoon baking soda

½ teaspoon salt

FLUFFY MARSHMALLOW CREAM:

⅓ cup water

¾ cup sugar

¾ cup corn syrup

3 egg whites

½ teaspoon cream of tartar

1 teaspoon pure vanilla extract

RICH CHOCOLATE GANACHE:

12 ounces semi-sweet chocolate chips, chopped (I used Hershey's)

2¼ cups heavy whipping cream

Directions

MAPLE CANDIED BACON:

1. Preheat oven to 375°F.

2. Cover a large baking pan with heavy duty foil and top with a baking rack. Lay the strips of bacon in a single layer on the baking rack.

3. Drizzle half of the pure maple syrup over the bacon and sprinkle with half of the light brown sugar.

4. Bake 15 minutes, or until bacon is cooked on one side. Turn over and drizzle with the remaining maple syrup and sprinkle the remaining light brown sugar over the top. Cook another 15 minutes, watching carefully not to burn edges. Remove outside pieces when done early, if needed. Remove from baking sheet to a pan or plate and allow to cool. They will firm up when cooled.

HOMEMADE BACON HONEY GRAHAM CRACKERS:

1. Reduce heat of the oven to 350°F. Line 2 sheet pans with parchment paper and set aside.

2. In a large skillet over medium heat, cook bacon pieces until done but not too dark, stirring occasionally. Remove with slotted spatula to a paper towel-lined pan. Chop finely and set aside. Remove 2 teaspoons of the bacon grease in the skillet to a small bowl to allow to cool while making dough.

3. In the bowl of a large food processor, pulse the butter and brown sugar until it resembles coarse crumbs. Add the honey, milk and pure vanilla extract and pulse to combine.

4. In a medium bowl, whisk the unbleached white flour, whole wheat flour, baking soda, and salt to combine. Gradually add to the mixture in the food processor, pulsing between additions. Add the chopped bacon and bacon grease and pulse to combine.

5. Remove the dough and divide into 2 balls. Wrap each ball in plastic wrap and refrigerate at least 10 minutes.

6. Roll the dough of the first ball on a lightly floured work surface until it is ⅛" thick, using flour on the rolling pin. Dip pig-shaped cookie cutters (2 large and 20 medium) into flour and cut shapes out of dough. Prick 5 times with a fork to resemble graham crackers. Transfer to the prepared baking sheets.

"As a contest cook, I spend hours, days, even months creating original recipes that become my cherished little babies. I'm proud of them, I adore them, and I want to share them with the world!"

—Paula Todora

DIRECTIONS CONTINUED

7. Bake 10 minutes, until barely brown. Remove from oven and allow to cool 5 minutes. Transfer cookies to a cooling rack with a spatula.

8. Repeat process with the second ball of dough.

FLUFFY MARSHMALLOW CREAM:

1. Over low heat in a saucepan, heat water, sugar, and corn syrup until the sugar is dissolved. Do not stir! Do not allow mixture to simmer until the sugar has fully dissolved, then turn to low, insert a candy thermometer into the saucepan, and cook until 240°F is reached. Remove from heat.

2. Making sure the mixing bowl is grease-free, beat egg whites and cream of tartar on high speed of an electric mixer until soft peaks form, about 3–4 minutes. Turn mixer speed to medium-low and pour the sugar syrup very slowly into the whites in a thin, steady stream. Turn speed to high and continue whipping 6–8 minutes until thick and glossy. Add vanilla and whip until the mixture is cooled completely.

RICH CHOCOLATE GANACHE:

1. Place chocolate chip pieces in a medium heat-proof bowl.

2. Over low heat in a medium saucepan, heat cream to a boil. Remove from heat and pour over chocolate chips, allowing it to stand for 3–4 minutes. Do not stir.

3. Starting in the middle of the bowl, whisk slowly and continue whisking in one direction outwards until it is smooth and glossy.

ASSEMBLY:

1. For each s'more, place one graham cracker on a flat surface. Spread generously with marshmallow fluff. Toast fluff lightly with a culinary torch on sides and top.

2. Add 2 slices of candied bacon in a crisscross fashion, allowing bacon to hang off edges of each graham cracker.

3. Generously top bacon with ganache, allowing it to gently drip down sides, and apply some to the edges of the bacon. Top with the second graham cracker.

4. Makes 12-20 s'mores (depending on sizes of cookie cutters).

Head Cook:
Jennifer Norem

Team Name:
Chef Jen & Team Indiana

Instagram:
@ChefJenNorem_74

A homemade, roasted garlic chipotle, deep-fried, puffy corn tortilla, filled with juicy bacon and poblano meatballs, covered in a spicy red chili sauce, and blanketed with gooey melted queso cheese. Graciously garnished with a cool lime crema, pickled salsa, and bacon crumbles.

Cook Time 45 Minutes | Make 4–6 servings

Ingredients

1 gallon peanut oil (for frying)

Tortilla press

Gallon freezer bag

ROASTED GARLIC CHIPOTLE CORN TORTILLAS:

7½ ounces chipotle peppers in adobo sauce

6 cloves garlic, roasted

2 cups instant corn masa

1½ cups water

2 teaspoons kosher salt

BACON POBLANO MEATBALLS:

1 16-ounce package hickory smoked bacon, finely chopped

2½ pounds ground chuck

2 cups chili cheese chips, finely crushed (I used Fritos)

2 poblano peppers, roasted, seeded and finely chopped

2 jalapeños, half seeded and finely chopped

1 small white onion, finely chopped

½ cup finely chopped cilantro

4 garlic cloves, minced

2 eggs

2 teaspoons kosher salt

1 teaspoon ground black pepper

PICKLED SALSA:

1 large red onion, halved and thinly sliced

1 bunch cilantro, coarsely chopped

1 10.5-ounce cherub tomatoes, cut into quarters

½ pound red radishes, julienne cut

1 tablespoon garlic olive oil

¼ cup red wine vinegar

1 teaspoon kosher salt

½ teaspoon fresh ground black pepper

RED CHILE SAUCE:

14½ ounces crushed tomatoes (I used Red Gold Chili Ready)

½ cup enchilada sauce

1 tablespoon granulated sugar

1 teaspoon red chile powder

2 teaspoons garlic powder

1 teaspoon cumin

LIME CREMA:

16 ounces sour cream

1 lime, juiced

1 tablespoon lime zest

1 teaspoon kosher salt

GARNISH:

1 cup crumbled hickory bacon

1–2 pounds shredded queso quesadilla cheese

TIP:

- You can substitute instant corn masa with finely ground cornmeal.

Directions

1. **Prepare roasted garlic chipotle corn tortillas:**

2. In a food processor, add two chipotle peppers, two tablespoons of adobo sauce from chipotle peppers, the six roasted garlic cloves, and olive oil. Pulsate until ingredients are completely smooth and contain no chunks.

3. In a medium-size mixing bowl, add the masa, water, salt, and the processed chipotle mixture. Completely mix until all ingredients are fully incorporated. Knead for about 3 to 5 minutes. Form masa into ball and wrap tightly in plastic wrap and set aside.

4. **Prepare red chile sauce:**

5. Add all ingredients to a medium saucepan over low heat. Cover and let simmer while preparing and cooking meatballs.

6. **Prepare bacon poblano meatballs:**

7. In a large mixing bowl, add all ingredients. Mix well until they are fully incorporated, but do not over mix. Form 1–1½" balls until all meat mixture is gone. Heat a large skillet with 1 teaspoon olive oil over medium heat. You may fit as many meatballs in the pan as you can. If you have leftovers, cook in another batch. Cook meatballs until browned on all sides, about 5 minutes or so. Cover and let cook over low heat until middles are done, about 10–15 minutes.

8. **Prepare pickled salsa:**

9. Combine all ingredients in a medium bowl and toss lightly, coating all ingredients. Cover and set aside.

10. **Prepare lime cream:**

11. In a small bowl, add all ingredients and stir well. Refrigerate until ready to use.

12. When meatballs are done, gently transfer them into the red chile sauce. Continue to cook on low heat, occasionally picking up saucepan and giving them a light whirl to avoid sticking to bottom or burning.

13. It's time to make the delicious homemade corn tortillas! With the masa, form masa into 2-inch balls, one at a time. Try to keep the other masa covered, as it will dry out quickly. Using your gallon bag, cut at least a 5-inch square out of the middle, so that you end up with two plastic squares. Use one plastic square to cover bottom of tortilla press.

14. In middle of tortilla press, place 2-inch masa ball, add other plastic

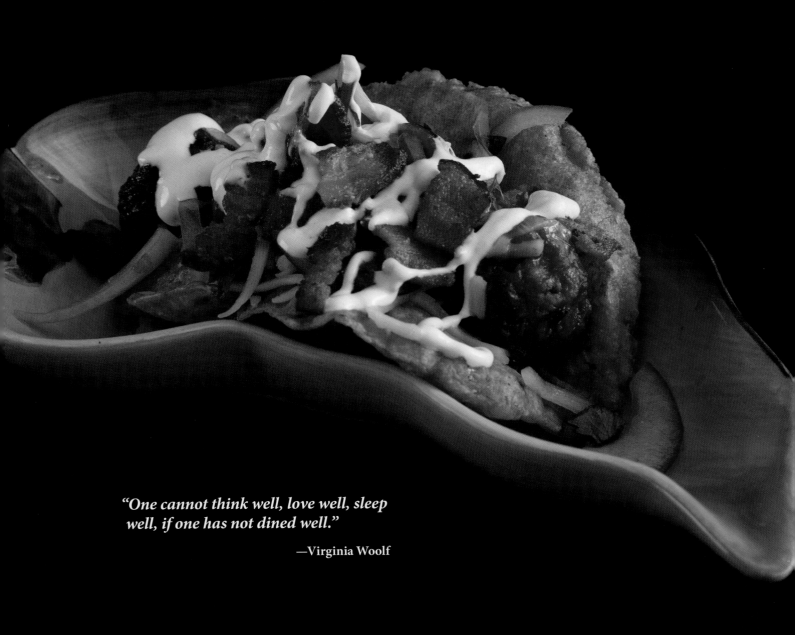

"One cannot think well, love well, sleep well, if one has not dined well."

—Virginia Woolf

DIRECTIONS CONTINUED

square to top of ball, and close press to create your tortilla. Make one at a time. Cook each tortilla on a comal. Repeat until you have made and cooked the desired amount of tortillas.

15. In a heavy-duty saucepan, fill with peanut oil until you have about 3 inches of oil. Heat oil on medium heat to 250°F. Once oil is hot, work with one tortilla at a time. Carefully place tortilla into oil and just as the tortilla begins to puff up, turn over in oil. With a non-melting spatula, carefully place spatula in center of the tortilla to help form the shape of a taco, about 1 to 2 minutes to brown and crisp up. Remove and let

drain on paper towel. Repeat steps for each tortilla until you reach your desired amount.

16. Now for the finished product, take one shell and add 2 to 3 meatballs, depending on the size of your meatballs. Add a generous amount of queso cheese, top with pickled salsa, lime crema, bacon crumbles and pork belly bits. Repeat, serve, and enjoy!

Double-Glazed Bacon Ramen

Head Cook:
Linwood Kennedy

Team Name:
The Avengers
Atlanta, GA

Business Name:
Eliza Soul Food Catering

Facebook:
Eliza Soul Food

Instagram:
@Chef_Ken1985

www.ElizaSoulFood.com

Who doesn't love bacon with ramen? This recipe infuses the two into one mighty combo.

Cook Time: 3 Hours, 45 Minutes | Makes 4 servings

Ingredients

RAMEN:

4 cups water

2 cloves garlic, peeled and smashed

3¼ slices ginger, peeled

6 slices bacon

2–3 tablespoons vegetable or olive oil for frying

2 tablespoons soy sauce

1 tablespoon mirin

Salt, to taste

2 packages ramen noodles

1 green onion, sliced

1 soft-boiled egg

PORK BRINE:

1½ pounds pork belly

¾ cup brown sugar

¾ cup sea salt

4 garlic cloves, crushed

1 teaspoon whole black peppercorn

2 cloves

1 bay leaf

1 thyme sprig

Directions

PORK BRINE:

1. Mix salt and sugar. Rub pork belly on all sides. Cover and refrigerate for 6-24 hours (overnight is perfect). Wipe off excess cure.

2. Preheat oven to 450°F. Roast pork belly, fat side up, for 45 minutes. Baste with own juices halfway through. Reduce heat to 250°F and roast an additional 1 hour 15 minutes. Remove from oven. (**Note:** These steps may be done up to three days in advance. Wrap belly tightly in plastic wrap and refrigerate until ready to use.)

3. If using belly the day of roasting, wrap it in plastic wrap and place in the freezer for 30–60 minutes to make slicing easier. Remove from refrigerator/freezer and unwrap. Slice to ¼" thickness. Fry for about 2 minutes per side in lightly oiled cast-iron pan until brown and slightly crispy. Remove to paper towel-lined plate until ready to assemble ramen.

RAMEN:

1. Combine water, garlic, ginger, and bacon in a medium saucepan over high heat. Bring to a boil and reduce heat to a strong simmer/low boil. Let cook together for 30 minutes.

2. Strain out aromatics and bacon and separate boiled bacon. Discard ginger and garlic.

3. In a skillet over medium heat, add a glug of oil and fry bacon until browned. Add salt to re-flavor your bacon. Remove from heat and slice into bite-size pieces.

4. Add soy sauce and mirin to broth then salt to taste.

5. Place noodles in serving bowl and ladle broth over.

6. Add pork belly. Garnish with remaining and other desired toppings of your choice and serve.

"One of the very nicest things about life is the way
we must regularly stop whatever it is we are doing
and devote our attention to eating."

—Luciano Pavarotti

Grilled Cheese and Tomato Soup

Head Cook:
Wayne Cooper

Team Name:
Blazed and Confused
Robert, LA

Facebook:
Wayne Cooper

Joseph Bruno, BeBe Anderson, Bo Johnson, and myself cooked in the World Food Championships in the Bacon category in 2018 and we took sixth place. Not bad when facing 50 of the top cooking teams in the world! So, we moved on to the next round, cooking against the other top ten competitors from round one. We were in full celebration mode that night, but we also had to make a plan for the next day because we didn't come prepared with a recipe in case we moved up.

A few years earlier, we were cooking in a qualifying event for the World Food Championships. Mike McCloud was there and sat at our table the evening before at the welcome party. We talked about many things that night, but what we remember the most was these words: "Keep it simple." Those words were spoken that night as we gathered to talk about a recipe, so we almost instantly agreed on this simple dish, a grilled cheese and tomato soup; about as simple as it gets.

Joe gets credit, as he's one awesome soup man. We ironed it out in a few minutes and made a trip to the grocery store. The battle started and we produced a dish that was amazing. When the dust settled, we moved up one spot to 5th. Middle of the pack against 9 world-class competitors.

Cook Time: 1 Hour | Makes 4–6 servings

Ingredients

SAVORY JAM:

1 tablespoon garlic powder

1 tablespoon balsamic vinegar

2 teaspoon herbes de Provence

1 cup onion, caramelized

1 cup garlic, roasted

3 8-ounce cans diced tomatoes (I used Red Gold Diced Tomatoes with Peppers)

Salt and pepper, to taste

CANDIED BACON AND GRILLED CHEESE:
(Ingredients per sandwich)

2 slices Muenster cheese

2 slices smoked provolone cheese

2 slices Texas toast

1 tablespoon butter

2 slices candied bacon (see ingredients below)

2 teaspoon brown sugar

1 pinch cayenne pepper

TOMATO SOUP:

¼ cup olive oil

4 cloves garlic

1 medium yellow onion, diced

2 carrots, diced

3 pounds Roma tomatoes

4 ounces fresh basil

½ ounces fresh oregano

1 tablespoon parmesan Reggiano cheese

2 quarts cream

Tomato paste (small can)

CREME FRAICHE:

1 cup sour cream

1 large lemon (juiced)

Directions

SAVORY JAM:

1. Heat olive oil and onions in sauté pan until caramelized.
2. Cut off tops of garlic cloves and coat in oil. Cover with foil and roast until tender.
3. Puree garlic.
4. Mix all ingredients together and simmer until it reaches jam consistency.

CANDIED BACON AND GRILLED CHEESE:

1. Preheat oven to 350°F and place bacon on parchment paper on sheet tray.
2. Mix together cayenne pepper and brown sugar.
3. Coat bacon and cook in oven for 25 minutes.
4. Brush melted butter on Texas toast.
5. Layer cheese, bacon, tomato jam, and cheese between bread.
6. Cook in cast iron skillet with plenty of butter until cheese is melted and you get a golden-brown crust.

TOMATO SOUP:

1. Toss Roma tomatoes in olive oil and char over grill. Place in brown bag to steam for 10 minutes. Pull skin off and deseed, then dice.
2. Dice carrots and sauté with onions, garlic, and tomato paste for 10 minutes. Cook until tender.
3. Add tomatoes to onion, garlic, and carrot mix.
4. Chiffonade basil and mince oregano.
5. Add cream to tomato and carrot mix, and simmer for 20 minutes.
6. Add basil and oregano, and simmer for 15 minutes.
7. Puree with stick mixer and strain.
8. Serve in bowl and garnish with creme fraiche and parmesan mix.

CREME FRAICHE:

1. Mix ingredients together.
2. Dollop as soup garnish.

"Turn me over, I am done on that side."

–Saint Lawrence

This is a decadent chocolate bacon Twinkie cake filled with peanut butter on top of bacon salted caramel. The Twinkie is drizzled with a bacon chocolate ganache and a bacon-cookie crumble mixture for crunch. Bacon peanut butter cream cheese icing is piped on top and studded with a chocolate caramel macaron and brûléed bacon.

My favorite part is the bacon icing, which is made with bacon powdered sugar. As far as I know, I invented bacon-powdered sugar, which led to the creation of the Bacon Twinkie. The cake is based on my favorite chocolate cake recipe, and the brûléed bacon is delicious on its own, but makes a great garnish for this dessert. I have used the base chocolate cake recipe on TV before. It was something that I made on *The Great American Baking Show* and also on *Good Morning America*, so it's definitely a staple of my baking repertoire.

Head Cook:
Lauren Katz

Team Name:
The Difference Baker
Ashburn, VA

Business Name:
The Difference Baker

Facebook:
Clouds of Cream

Instagram:
@LaurenK_Bakes

Cook Time: 1 Hour | Makes 10–12 cakes

Ingredients

TWINKIE CAKES:

1 cup flour

1 cup sugar

⅓ cup plus 1 tablespoon dark cocoa powder

1 teaspoon baking soda

½ teaspoon baking powder

¼ teaspoon bacon salt

8 slices cooked crispy bacon, finely chopped or crumbled

1 egg

1 teaspoon vanilla extract or paste

½ cup vegetable oil

½ cup sour cream

½ cup brewed coffee

BACON CARAMEL:

¾ cup prepared salted caramel (from a jar)

2–3 tablespoons rendered bacon fat

Pinch bacon salt

BACON POWDERED SUGAR:

8 strips microwaved bacon, crispy and as dry as possible

1–½ cups powdered sugar

BACON PEANUT BUTTER ICING:

1 block cream cheese, room temperature

1 stick unsalted butter, room temperature

2 tablespoons brown sugar

1–1¼ cups bacon powdered sugar (recipe below)

2 tablespoons creamy peanut butter

1 teaspoon vanilla extract or paste

BACON CHOCOLATE GANACHE:

6 ounces heavy cream

6 ounces semi-sweet chocolate chips

⅛ teaspoon bacon salt

1 tablespoon rendered bacon fat

BRÛLÉED BACON:

5 pieces of cooked bacon, cut in half

2 tablespoons maple syrup

Pinch cayenne pepper

Pinch chili powder

Turbinado sugar (to coat)

Directions

1. Preheat oven to 325°F. Cook chopped and whole bacon on stovetop in two pans. Once cooked, reserve fat.

TWINKIE CAKES:

1. Prepare a 12 Twinkie pan with non-stick spray (or these can be made as cupcakes in a lined muffin tin).

2. Whisk to combine the dry ingredients in a mixing bowl. Combine remaining wet ingredients in a measuring cup and pour into center of dry ingredients. Mix well and spoon or pipe into prepared pan, filling each cavity half full.

3. Bake for 12–16 minutes or until just done in center. Let cool on wire rack.

BACON CARAMEL:

1. In a small bowl, whisk all caramel ingredients together and set aside in a piping bag or squeeze bottle.

BACON POWDERED SUGAR:

1. In a food processor, process the cooled, microwaved bacon and powdered sugar to create as fine a powder as possible. Set aside.

BACON PEANUT BUTTER ICING:

1. Combine all ingredients with electric mixer until smooth and airy. Set aside in piping bag.

BACON CHOCOLATE GANACHE:

1. Heat cream until just under a boil on the stovetop or in a measuring cup in the microwave.

2. Add chocolate chips and let sit for 3 minutes.

3. Whisk gently to combine until all chocolate melts.

4. Whisk in the bacon fat and salt. Set aside until ready to use.

BRÛLÉED BACON:

1. Place cooked bacon on a foil-lined baking sheet.

DIRECTIONS CONTINUED

2. In a small bowl, combine maple syrup, cayenne, and chili powder.

3. Brush maple syrup mixture onto each bacon slice.

4. Sprinkle evenly with a coat of turbinado sugar.

5. Brûlée with a torch or carefully under the broiler until sugar melts and turns golden brown. Let cool until crisped.

ASSEMBLY:

1. Fill cooled twinkies with icing.

2. Top with more icing, piped in swirls.

3. Drizzle with ganache and caramel.

4. Top with a piece of brûléed bacon and a store-bought chocolate macaron (if desired).

"I would encourage anyone to start baking, even if you're not comfortable with being in the kitchen. The way to get better is by practicing and spending time experimenting in the kitchen."

—Lauren Katz

Maple-Glazed Peaches and Cream
Bacon Burnt Ends Sliders

Head Cook:
Scott Carlisle

Team Name:
Lucky Shoes BBQ
Dennison, MN

Business Name:
Lucky Shoes BBQ

Facebook:
@LuckyShoesBBQ

Instagram:
@LuckyShoesBBQ

TikTok:
@LuckyShoesBBQ

These delicious sliders will score big on appearances with their maple-glazed Hawaiian buns sprinkled with candied bacon. The peach and sweet onion jam adds a savory element to the sandwich while the jalapeño bacon aioli brings a creamy texture. The star of the show is the pile of jalapeño-peach glazed bacon burnt ends. This recipe brings a lot of big flavors and textures that complement the abundance of bacon in this dish. Cook these sliders at the next get-together and they are sure to be a big hit!

Cook Time: 1 Hour, 30 Minutes | Makes 12 servings

Ingredients

4 pounds bacon (2 pounds diced and 2 pounds 1-inch cubed)

1 pound peaches

4 jalapeños, sliced

3 onions, sliced

2 garlic cloves, finely diced

1 lemon

1 pinch thyme

1 pinch chives

1 cup mayonnaise

2 tablespoons candied jalapeños, diced

½ cup peach nectar

3 tablespoons milk

½ teaspoon maple extract

½ cup sugar

½ cup maple sugar

2 cups confectioner's sugar

2 cups maple syrup

3 tablespoons chili jelly (I used Hassel Cattle Company Wagyu Bacon & Hatch Chili Jelly)

12 buns

Salt, to taste

Pepper, to taste

Directions

1. Candy the bacon lardon with sugars and maple syrup on stove on low heat for about an hour.

2. Mix 1 cup confectioner's sugar, 1 tablespoon maple syrup, ¼ teaspoon maple extract, and 2 tablespoons milk for glaze.

3. Glaze buns with maple glaze and sprinkle candied bacon on top.

4. Cook peaches, peach nectar, jalapeños, maple syrup, maple sugar, and sugar on stove on low heat for about an hour or until slightly thickened for sauce.

5. Bake bacon burnt ends in oven at 400°F until nearly finished, about 45 minutes. Glaze with peach sauce and bake until sauce sets, about 15 minutes.

6. Mix mayonnaise, chili jelly, herbs, lemon juice, and candied jalapeños for aioli.

7. Slow cook on low heat onions, garlic, peaches, maple syrup, sugars, bacon on stove for jam for about an hour.

8. Construct slider and chow down!

"Nothing brings people together better than a BBQ!"

—Scott Carlisle

Head Cook:
Mark Emery

Team Name:
Spark
Bentonville, AR

Inspired by a classic BLT, our signature bacon dish is amped up with whole braised bacon slabs, crisp iceberg, ripe tomato steaks, all between a toasted bacon brioche bread. Not to be outdone, it also includes bacon fries, a custom spicy ketchup, and a tasty vinegar and oil coleslaw.

Cook Time: 1 Hour, 45 Minutes | Makes 4–6 servings

Ingredients

SPICY BRAISED BACON SLAP:

Uncut slab applewood smoked bacon

½ slab pork belly

1 liter soda (I used Sam's Cola)

1 can chipotle peppers in adobo sauce

2 cans petite diced tomatoes and green chilies (I used Red Gold)

1 can tomato sauce (I used Red Gold Chili Ready)

Canola oil

SWEET BRAISED BACON:

Uncut slab sugar cured smoked bacon

½ slab pork belly

1 liter soda (I used Sam's Cola)

1 can tomato sauce (I used Red Gold Chili Ready)

1 can crushed tomatoes (I used Red Gold Chili Ready)

Canola oil

BACON GARNISH:

12 ounces thick cut applewood bacon

½ cup maple syrup

Cooking spray

BACON FRIES:

1 gallon canola oil

10 small Idaho russet potatoes

1 packet dry ranch seasoning packet (I used Hidden Valley)

12 ounces hickory smoked bacon, precooked and chopped

1 bunch fresh parsley, chopped

CUSTOM KETCHUP:

1 cup ketchup

¼ cup reserved spicy braising liquid (made from Spicy Braised Bacon Slap recipe)

CUSTOM BACONNAISE:

4 slices applewood bacon

2 ounces diced onion

2 ounces diced carrots

2 ounces diced celery

1¼ cup mayonnaise

¼ cup apple cider vinegar

½ teaspoon ground turmeric

Ice (for ice bath)

1 gallon water (for ice bath)

VINEGAR AND OIL COLESLAW:

5 multicolor fresh bell peppers

⅓ cup apple cider vinegar

½ cup maple syrup

2 packages shredded multicolor cabbage

1 tablespoon prepared horseradish

¼ teaspoon celery seed

½ teaspoon celery salt

Salt and pepper, to taste

ADDITIONAL INGREDIENTS:

8 heads iceberg lettuce

8 beefsteak tomatoes

11 green onions

1 bunch fresh parsley

3 loaves brioche bread

Directions

1. Instructions below are for a BLT sandwich and supporting sides and sauces. Components will build to a point and then combined at the end during the final build of the dish.
2. Preheat oven to 500°F.

SPICY BRAISED BACON SLAP:

1. Combine soda, chipotle peppers in adobo, petite diced tomatoes with green chilies, and tomato sauce.
2. Add applewood smoked slab to pressure cooker with all ingredients.

3. Put on burner and bring up full steam. Turn down cooker and cook for 18 minutes.
4. Rest off heat. Open up cooker.
5. Set bacon aside, add remaining sauce to a blender, and blend. Then set aside.
6. Slice pork belly to ½"-inch cubes, flash fry until crisp, 6 pieces at a time, for 5 minutes at 375°F in canola oil. Set aside for sandwich build.
7. Reserve braising liquid.

SWEET BRAISED BACON:

1. Combine soda, tomato sauce, and crushed tomatoes.
2. Add sugar-cured slab to pressure cooker with all ingredients.
3. Put on burner and bring to full steam. Turn down cooker and cook for 18 minutes.
4. Rest off heat. Open up cooker.
5. Set bacon aside, add remaining sauce to a blender and blend. Then set aside.

DIRECTIONS CONTINUED

6. Slice pork belly to ½"-cubes, flash fry until crisp, 6 pieces at a time, for 5 minutes at 375°F in canola oil. Set aside for sandwich build.

7. Reserve braising liquid.

BACON GARNISH:

1. Lay out 12 ounces applewood bacon on a wire rack over baking pan. Brush with ¼ cup maple syrup.

2. Place in oven at 500°F. Cook until done on one side (approximately 20 minutes).

3. Flip bacon and brush with remaining ¼ cup maple syrup.

4. Remove from oven and set aside for coleslaw and sandwich skewer garnish.

BACON FRIES:

1. Add oil to pot for frying. Heat.

2. Scrub and clean potatoes, cut into 6 wedges.

3. Check oil is heating.

4. Place whole cut wedges in pressure cooker with chopped, precooked, thick cut bacon and a pinch of dry ranch seasoning.

5. Heat pressure cooker to full steam, turn down pressure cooker, cook for 10 minutes.

6. Take cooker off heat and let cool. Remove potatoes from pot and let cool at room temperature for 10 minutes.

7. Wrap each wedge in ½ piece of precooked bacon.

8. Fry at 375°F until fully crisp.

9. Garnish with additional ranch seasoning and chopped parsley.

CUSTOM KETCHUP:

1. Combine well ketchup and reserved spicy braising liquid. Add to deli squeeze bottle.

CUSTOM BACONNAISE:

1. Add applewood bacon, roughly chopped, to a small sauté pan and cook. Once cooked, approximately 6 minutes, add chopped onion, carrots, and celery.

2. Cook bacon mirepoix (vegetables) over medium heat until translucent.

3. Deglaze pan with apple cider vinegar. Set mixture aside and cool in ice bath.

4. Add materials to food processor and purée until smooth.

5. Remove blade, add mayonnaise and turmeric. Fold until well combined.

6. Set mayonnaise mixture aside.

VINEGAR AND OIL COLESLAW:

1. Clean and prepare multicolored bell peppers. Quarter three of them. Julienne a fourth and set aside. Brunoise a fifth and set aside (for garnish.)

2. Prepare cabbage dressing including vinegar, maple syrup, horseradish, celery seed, celery salt, and salt and pepper to taste.

3. Combine dressing with chopped cabbage.

4. Add maple bacon garnish just before service.

THICK CUT LETTUCE STEAKS:

1. Clean and remove outer layers of 8 heads of iceberg lettuce.

2. Cut 11 tight lettuce steaks.

3. Brush with ambient temperature bacon fat and season with salt and pepper.

4. Set aside.

BEEFSTEAK TOMATOES:

1. Wash 6 tomatoes.

2. Cut into 12 slices at ⅜".

3. Place in hotel pan with sweet braising liquid.

BACON VEGGIE GARNISH SKEWER:

1. Clean and prepare 11 green onions, cut bottom off and flower.

2. Place in ice bath to expand. Set aside.

3. Fine cut parsley and green onion tips. Combine and set aside.

4. Build skewer for sandwich prepared green onion, jarred red pepper, maple bacon garnish.

TOASTED BREAD:

1. Clean and trip crust from loaves of brioche bread. Select best 16 slices.

2. Toast for color on grill or cast-iron pan.

3. Set aside on wire rack.

4. Brush with bacon grease.

5. Bake in oven at 500°F to continue to toast.

ASSEMBLY:

1. Prepare full sandwich. Starting from the bottom up: brioche toast, mayo spread, lettuce steak, 2 bacon slabs of each flavor, tomato steak, mayo spread, brioche toast, garnish skewer above.

2. Add to plate a small dish of prepared coleslaw garnished with maple bacon.

3. Add 2–3 bacon-wrapped fries to each dish.

4. Use squirt bottle to tastefully add spicy ketchup.

5. Garnish appropriately with green onion/parsley blend and julienne/brunoise bell peppers.

Pearls Before Swine

Head Cook:
Jodi Taffel

Team Name:
The Fabulous Bacon Babe
Monrovia, CA

Business Name:
Bacon Babe Catering

Facebook:
Jodi Taffel; Bacon Babe Catering

Instagram:
@The.Bacon.Babe

Tonkatsu-braised bacon steak dredged in panko and bacon crumbs, then fried to a golden brown in bacon liquid gold with homemade, Asian-inspired sweet and spicy chili sauce and garnished with bacon snow and ponzu pearls. I can't really describe my inspiration behind any dish, to be frank, because I never know when inspiration will hit. Sometimes I'm inspired by a particular ingredient. Sometimes I'm inspired by something I see on television or in a restaurant. Sometimes it's as simple as finding a plate that I really like and want to use.

Cook Time: 1 Hour | Makes 4–6 servings

Ingredients

TONKATSU BRAISED BACON STEAKS:

2 packages hickory smoked bacon (I used Pederson's Natural Farms No Sugar Added)

3 pounds slab bacon

2 packets tonkatsu broth concentrate

2 packets shoyu broth concentrate

6 cups water

2 tablespoons Shaoxing wine

1 tablespoon Chinese five-spice powder

1 teaspoon white pepper

1 cup all-purpose flour

2 eggs

1 tablespoon water

1 cup panko crumbs

½ cup canola oil

1 teaspoon salt

1 bunch chives (garnish)

Microgreens/flowers (garnish)

ASIAN-INSPIRED SWEET & SPICY CHILI SAUCE:

½ cup rice wine vinegar

1 cup + 2 tablespoons water

⅔ cup white sugar

¼ cup garlic, minced

1 tablespoon dark soy sauce

3 tablespoons chili garlic sauce

4 tablespoons cornstarch

PONZU PEARLS:

4 cups grapeseed oil

1 cup ponzu sauce

1 tablespoon agar-agar

1 cup cold water

BACON SNOW:

2 tablespoons rendered bacon fat

1 cup tapioca maltodextrin

Directions

TONKATSU BRAISED BACON STEAKS:

1. Roughly chop 1 package of sliced bacon and add to a soup pot with the broth concentrates and water. Bring to a boil.
2. Cut slab bacon into 1-inch thick slices and add to broth.
3. Reduce to a simmer and allow to braise 45 minutes.
4. Roughly chop the 2nd package of sliced bacon and cook until crisp.
5. Set rendered bacon fat aside.
6. Set aside ¼ of the cooked bacon. Chop the remaining bacon a bit finer.
7. Set up 3 dredging stations: 1 flour, 1 egg wash, 1 panko mixed with finely chopped bacon.
8. Remove slab bacon from broth. Do not pat dry.
9. Dredge in flour, egg wash, panko.
10. Add vegetable oil and the saved bacon fat to a sauté pan and heat until it glistens.
11. Fry 1–2 minutes per side, or until golden.
12. Transfer to paper towel lined plate to drain off excess oil and sprinkle with salt.
13. Chop remaining cooked bacon finer and set aside.
14. Finely chop chives and set aside.

ASIAN-INSPIRED SWEET & SPICY CHILI SAUCE:

1. Bring rice wine vinegar, ¾ cup water, sugar, garlic, and soy sauce to a boil, making sure all the sugar is dissolved. Allow to boil about 1 minute once sugar is dissolved.
2. Add chili garlic sauce and stir continuously to thoroughly combine everything. Allow to boil an additional minute.
3. Mix cornstarch with 2 tablespoons water to create a slurry and add to the mixture.
4. Once the slurry is thoroughly incorporated, turn off heat and mix in remaining ¼ cup water.
5. Push through a fine mesh sieve into a clean bowl to remove any slurry bits that clumped up.

BACON SNOW:

1. If not still liquid, melt bacon fat over medium heat.
2. Whisk in tapioca maltodextrin until mixture becomes a powder.

TIPS:

- Shoyu is Japanese for soy sauce.
- You can substitute Shaoxing wine with cooking wine.

*"If you're afraid of butter,
just use cream."*

—Julia Child

DIRECTIONS CONTINUED

3. Push through a fine mesh sieve.

PONZU PEARLS:

1. Nest 4 small metal bowls inside 4 larger metal bowls filled with ice. Pour ½ cup grapeseed oil into each of the 4 small bowls. Set aside to chill.

2. Place ponzu sauce in a medium-sized saucepan and bring to a boil.

3. Add agar-agar and bring back to a boil.

4. Using a pipette or squeeze bottle with a small opening, suck up the liquid and drop by drops into the ice-cold oil. (This creates the pearls).

Allow to sit in the oil undisturbed until ready to plate.

5. Strain pearls from the oil and transfer to the cold water.

6. Strain pearls from water.

ASSEMBLY:

1. Make a puddle of chili sauce on each plate.

2. Place 1 piece of fried bacon in the middle of the sauce puddle.

3. Sprinkle the top with bacon snow.

4. Top with a heaping spoonful of bacon pearls.

5. Garnish with reserved chopped bacon, chives, and microgreens/flowers.

Head Cook:
Tore Trupiano

Team Name:
Mangia e Bevi
Oceanside, CA

Business Name:
Dominic's Italian Restaurant;
D'Vino Wine Bar & Cafe

Instagram:
@natores

Pan seared salmon with sauteed broccolini, puttanesca sauce with bacon lardons, basil gremolata, shaved fennel, and bacon nest.

Cook Time: 45 Minutes | Makes 4–6 servings

Ingredients

BROCCOLINI:

15 broccolini

Salt and pepper, to taste

1 tablespoon EVOO

GREMOLATA:

6 basil leaves

2 cloves garlic

1 bunch parsley

1 cup extra-virgin olive oil

PUTTANESCA SAUCE:

1 lemon

1 red onion, julienne cut

4 cloves garlic, minced

2 pounds thick cut bacon

14½ ounces petite diced tomatoes (I used Red Gold Tomatoes with Green Chilies)

1 cup mixed olives

½ cup capers

14½ ounces San Marzano tomatoes, puréed

Sea salt, to taste

1 teaspoon basil

1 teaspoon tomato paste

¼ cup white wine

Salt and pepper, to taste

Olive oil for sautéing

SALMON:

3 pounds salmon

Rendered bacon grease

1 tablespoon extra-virgin olive oil

Salt and pepper, to taste

FENNEL NEST:

1 bulb fennel

¼ cup fronds

1 tablespoon EVOO

3 slices bacon, cooked and crumbled

GARNISH:

4 radishes, thinly sliced

Directions

BROCCOLINI:

1. Blanche broccolini in salted water until tender.
2. Remove and place on paper towels to dry.
3. Sauté broccolini with salt, pepper, extra virgin olive oil, and bacon fat.

GREMOLATA:

1. Finely chop basil, parsley, and garlic mixed with olive oil to create gremolata.

PUTTANESCA SAUCE:

1. Sauté red onion with olive oil.
2. Add garlic and sauté until translucent and aromatic.
3. Cut bacon into small pieces. Sauté and separate bacon renderings and grease.
4. Strain petite diced tomatoes with green chilies, separate juice and reserve.
5. Hand tear olives into small pieces.
6. Desalt capers in fresh water.

7. Cut lemon in half and add juice of half a lemon to puttanesca sauce.
8. Add Capers and olives.
9. Add petite diced tomatoes with green chilies.
10. Add a little of the tomato juice from reserve.
11. Add puréed San Marzano tomatoes with sea salt and basil and a teaspoon of tomato paste.
12. Deglaze sauté pan with white wine.
13. Add salt and pepper cook on medium heat until puttanesca is reduced.
14. Add bacon to puttanesca sauce and basil chiffonade.

SALMON:

1. Heat bacon grease and extra virgin olive oil in a sauté pan.
2. Salt and pepper both sides of salmon fillet.
3. Place salmon skin side down in sauté pan.

4. Transfer salmon into the oven and bake until salmon releases automatically from the pan.
5. Turn and cook skin side up.

FENNEL NEST:

1. Shave fennel using a mandolin slicer.
2. And toss with fronds, EVOO, and bacon.

ASSEMBLY:

1. Plate broccolini, then salmon on top skin up.
2. Add puttanesca, gremolata around edges, and fennel nest.
3. Garnish with radish and parsnip coins.

"So long as you have food in your mouth you have solved all questions for the time being."

—Franz Kafka

Savory Bacon Bread Pudding Souffle
with Tomato Choron

Inspired by the eggs benedict served with a flakey pastry base at NOLO's Court of Two Sisters and her grandmother's bread pudding, this dish is a savory bacon bread pudding with spicy tomatoes, leeks and jalapeño. The bread puddings are baked in a cupcake tin to ensure each "base" of the benedicts are crispy on the outside with a creamy, cheesy filling. Topped with a perfectly poached egg, crispy bacon, and drenched with a spicy choron hollandaise, this dish will have you going back for more!

Prep Time: 20 Minutes | Cook Time: 1 Hour | Makes 10–12 servings

Head Cook:
Tamie Joeckel

Team Name:
Tamie Joeckel
Katy, TX

Instagram:
@FrillsAndMeals
www.TwoSouthernSisters.com

Ingredients

BACON BREAD PUDDING:

3 pounds bacon

12 cups French bread, cubed

16 eggs

2 cups half and half

4 cups heavy cream

2 14.5-ounce cans petite diced tomatoes, drained and squeeze out extra water (I used Red Gold Tex Mex Tomatoes)

1 tablespoon salt

1 tablespoon pepper

4 cups shredded Gouda cheese

2 cups shredded jalapeño Havarti cheese

1 cup diced leeks

2 jalapeños, diced

2 medium onions, finely diced

2 cloves garlic, finely minced

2 tablespoons butter

2 tablespoons bacon fat (reserved during recipe)

POACHED EGGS:

4 tablespoons white vinegar

12 eggs (for poaching)

CHORON HOLLANDAISE:

8 sticks unsalted butter

10 egg yolks (room temperature)

4 tablespoons Worcestershire sauce

4 tablespoons lemon juice

1 can 14.5-ounce can petite diced tomatoes, drain and squeeze out extra water (I used Red Gold Tex Mex Tomatoes)

1 teaspoon cayenne

BACON PARMESAN CRISPS:

4 tablespoons finely crushed bacon bits

2 cups shredded parmesan cheese

BACON SQUIGGLES GARNISH:

1 pound bacon

Directions

BACON BREAD PUDDING:

1. Preheat oven to 350°F. Bring eggs to room temperature.

2. Cut 3 pounds of bacon into ½" strips and cook in a large skillet until crispy. Set aside and drain, but reserve drippings. Reserve 4 tablespoons for parmesan crisps. (Use the other pound of bacon to make bacon garnishes.)

3. Place diced French bread on a cookie sheet and bake until barely browned in the 350°F oven, about 10 minutes. (**Tip**: Stale bread is best for bread puddings. Browning the bread in the oven dries out the bread and adds texture.)

4. In a large mixing bowl, whisk together eggs, half & half, cream, petite diced tomatoes, salt, and pepper. Add the bread and all cheeses, stir, and set aside.

5. Chop all veggies.

6. In another skillet, add butter and bacon drippings, and sauté veggies until tender. Add ½ teaspoon salt and ½ teaspoon pepper. Let cool slightly then fold this mixture into the bread mixture. Fold in all but 2 cups of the crispy bacon.

7. Spray large muffin tins with butter spray and place in oven to heat for about 12 minutes.

8. When the bread mixture is combined, fill each muffin tin. Make an indention in the middle top of each muffin to accommodate rising. Bake for 30 to 40 minutes until browned. Set aside.

BACON PARMESAN CRISPS:

1. Mix bacon bits with shredded parmesan.

2. Heap tablespoons of the mixture onto parchment paper and spread into 12 discs.

3. Bake until golden brown and take out to cool.

BACON SQUIGGLES:

1. Loop bacon on a wire rack pan and bake until crispy.

2. If you don't have a wire rack pan, just bake the bacon flat until crispy.

POACHED EGGS:

1. Fill a saucepan with approximately 4 inches of water and bring to a rolling boil.

2. Add white vinegar to the water and reduce heat to a gentle, steady boil.

3. To poach the eggs, break each egg into a cup or small bowl and gently pour into the water. With a slotted spoon, gently keep the egg whites together (the vinegar helps with this as well). Cook eggs approximately 3 minutes each. Remove from the water and drain on a flat paper towel.

I've never been more reminded of how important food is to our family traditions than when my son came home after a tour in Iraq. I got up early and started frying bacon for breakfast. Trey came downstairs and hugged me, saying that just the smell of the bacon cooking reminded him he was home and safe. I think it's so important to pass down our family recipes and holiday traditions to our future generations!"

—Tamie Joeckel

DIRECTIONS CONTINUED

CHORON HOLLANDAISE (BLENDER VERSION):

1. For the sauce, melt the butter in the microwave on high heat until hot and bubbly.

2. In a blender, add the room temperature egg yolks. Add cold water and pulse the egg yolks until frothy.

3. With the blender running on med-high speed, slowly drizzle the hot butter into the blender. (Make sure you get the milkfat!) You'll hear a distinct difference in the sauce as the yolks thicken.

4. Add the lemon juice and Worcestershire sauce.

5. Add petite diced tomatoes, cayenne pepper and blend. Set aside. (You can keep the sauce warm by placing the blender bowl in hot water in a large mixing bowl.) Sauce should be made immediately before serving. If it's too thick, add a little hot water.

ASSEMBLY:

1. To serve, place a bread pudding muffin on a plate or shallow bowl.

2. Place a poached egg on top and drizzle with choron sauce.

3. Crumble the bacon that's left and sprinkle on each.

4. Garnish with a parmesan crisp and bacon squiggle.

Head Cook:
Anna Saunders (Davis)

Team Name:
Chef Anna
Springfield, MO

Business Name:
Private Chef Anna

Facebook:
Chef Anna, Private Chef

www.PrivateChefAnna.com

Street food hits a special place in everyone's heart, and this dish is the epitome of that. A savory spin off the beignet, this dish of savory doughnuts is full of "cheesy baconness," hyped up with truffle honey bourbon glaze, candied bacon salsa, homestyle potato chips, and bacon chili aioli. Oh, and we can't forget that bourbon bacon butter!

Cook Time: 45 Minutes | Makes 6 servings

Ingredients

BACON CHEESE BEIGNETS:

1 loaf brioche bread

12 ounces aged Gouda cheese, grated

¼ cup reserved bacon grease

4 eggs

2 tablespoons sugar

1 clove garlic, grated

3 tablespoons half and half

3 tablespoons minced chives

8 ounces triple cream Brie

5 cups butter cracker crumbs

TRUFFLE CHIPS:

1 quart oil (for frying)

2 pounds fingerling potatoes

3 tablespoons dried parsley

2 teaspoons truffle salt

½ cup reserved bacon grease

3 bacon ends

CHILI AIOLI:

½ cup tomato sauce, divided (I used Red Gold Chili Ready Tomato Sauce)

6 tablespoons truffle honey, divided

2 egg yolks

1 tablespoon lemon juice

½ cup olive oil

BACON THREE WAYS:

1 pound maple bacon

½ pound thick cut bacon

½ pound bacon ends

1 tablespoon coffee grounds

1 tablespoon ground pepper

5 teaspoons golden balsamic vinegar, divided

5 tablespoons spicy chili jelly, divided

5 tablespoons bourbon, divided

2 medium heirloom tomatoes

10 sweet piquanté peppers

6 ounces blackberries

6 ounces butter

1 bunch chives, minced

TIP:

- You can substitute golden balsamic vinegar with rice vinegar.

Directions

1. Begin with ingredients listed in "Bacon Three Ways" recipe, cooking the maple bacon in a skillet on medium-high until crispy and render bacon grease from it. Set aside all grease to use throughout the recipe.
2. Cook thick cut bacon in a separate skillet. Reserve bacon grease and set aside.
3. Mix coffee grounds and ground pepper together. On a medium baking dish, place bacon ends. Rub with coffee and pepper mixture. Cook bacon ends in a pan in the oven for 30 minutes. Set aside.

BACON CHEESE BEIGNETS:

1. Heat a medium pot halfway full of oil. Meanwhile, cut the crust off the bread.
2. Crumble bread into a large bowl, and add 6 ounces of Gouda cheese, bacon grease, 2 eggs, chives, sugar, grated garlic, cream, and 1 teaspoon salt.
3. Mix together into one homogeneous mixture, but don't over mix. You want to still have lightness to the dough.

4. Form into 30 small balls. Set aside.
5. Cut Brie into 30 pieces.
6. Using your finger, press one into each dough ball roll back into shape.
7. Beat remaining 2 eggs in a medium bowl.
8. In a food processor, grind cracker crumbs until fine. Place in another medium bowl.
9. Dip balls in egg and then into cracker crumbs. Repeat.
10. Fry in hot oil until golden brown. Keep in a warm place until serving.

TRUFFLE CHIPS:

1. Using 2 cups of the oil used for beignets, add rendered bacon grease. Heat for frying.
2. Using a mandolin, slice fingerling potatoes into thin slices. Place immediately in cold water. Let them sit in water for a few minutes to reduce starch.
3. In a small bowl, mix dried parsley and truffle salt. Have an additional large bowl ready for tossing the chips in once they are done frying.

4. Drain the potato slices and fry in small batches. Once each batch is a nice light golden color, remove from the oil and toss with some truffle parsley salt. Set on a tray to fully cool. Repeat until all the chips are fried. When chips are done, fry three bacon ends. Set aside.

CHILI AIOLI:

1. Beat together egg yolks, lemon juice, 2 tablespoons tomato sauce, truffle zest salt, and 1 teaspoon truffle honey. Slowly drizzle in oil and 1 tablespoon bacon grease until thick.
2. Place in a squeeze bottle and set in a cool place until ready to serve.

BACON THREE WAYS:

Deep fried and glazed:

1. Mix together 3 tablespoons truffle honey, ¼ cup chili jelly, 3 tablespoons bourbon, and 1 teaspoon golden balsamic vinegar. Using the maple bacon cooked previously, toss glaze over bacon ends, remove, and keep warm.

"Food is more than taste. It's 100 percent flavor, 100 percent presentation, and 100 percent an unforgettable experience."

—Anna Saunders (Davis)

DIRECTIONS CONTINUED

Candied Bacon Salsa:

1. Dice tomatoes and piquanté peppers. Set aside. Dice the ½ pound of previously cooked, thick-cut bacon and return bacon pieces to a skillet to cook until crispy. Add 2 tablespoons of truffle honey and cook until candied. Stir in ¼ cup tomato sauce, 2 tablespoons chili jelly, 2 teaspoons vinegar, and the blackberries. Remove from heat and mix into the diced tomatoes and peppers.

Coffee-Rubbed Bacon Ends:

1. Completed at beginning of instructions.

BACON BOURBON BUTTER:

1. Brown butter in a small skillet. Once browned, add bourbon, ¼ cup reserved bacon grease, and 2 teaspoons vinegar whisk together and set aside.

GARNISHES:

1. Mince 1 bunch of chives, set aside.

2. Place extra-grated Gouda cheese on a baking sheet lined with parchment paper. Toast cheese and crush into a cheese powder. Set aside.

3. With a zester, grate the 3 pieces of the deep-fried bacon. Set aside.

ASSEMBLY:

1. Place five beignets on each plate and drizzle with brown butter.

2. Disperse glazed bacon around the edge.

3. Drizzle bacon aioli over everything.

4. Spoon a generous portion of bacon salsa in the center of each pile of beignets.

5. Pile with coffee-rubbed bacon ends and a handful of truffle chips.

6. Garnish with dots of bacon aioli, chives, bacon zest, and Gouda powder.

7. Enjoy!

Uptown Chicken Fried Bacon

Head Cook:
Deborah Thomas

Team Name:
Team Island View
Gulford, MS

After my high score with my Chicken Styled Fried Bacon the year before, I decided to elevate (Up Town) my recipe by changing a few ingredients. So, trying new style of things, such as quick pickling and combining texture with taste, gave me the idea for this dish. Choosing the best smokey applewood bacon plays a big part in this recipe. Combining smoked bacon rubbed with southern spices, sweet notes of fruits, and refreshing creamy cheese with textures and sour notes make your tastes buds sing. Crispy chicken-style fried bacon topped with a sweet fig caramelized onion and bacon jam, dressed with quick pickled okra and creamy marinated Australian goat and sheep cheese. Adding the pickled mustard seeds is optional, but adds texture and another flavor level.

Cook Time: 1 Hour, 30 Minutes | Makes 4–6 servings

Ingredients

SWEET FIG CARAMELIZED ONION BACON JAM:

¼ cup vegetable oil

2 cups diced onions

1 tablespoon coarse black pepper

1 tablespoon crushed red pepper flakes

½ teaspoon ground coriander

1 tablespoon minced garlic

2 cups quartered Black Mission figs

½ cup apple cider vinegar

2 cups brown sugar

1 pound bacon, diced

QUICK-PICKLED OKRA:

1 pound fresh okra

4 fresh garlic cloves

2 teaspoons pickling spice

1 basil sprig

1 oregano sprig

2 cups white vinegar

¼ cup sugar

½ cup water

1 tablespoon kosher salt

¼ teaspoon cayenne

QUICK-PICKLED MUSTARD SEEDS:

½ cup apple cider vinegar

½ cup water

3 tablespoons sugar

½ teaspoon kosher salt

⅓ cup yellow mustard seeds

1 small shallot, thinly sliced

BACON:

Applewood smoked bacon (I used Nueske's)

2 tablespoons smoked seasoning rub

2 cups flour

Chicken fry breading (I used Zatarains)

4 eggs, beaten

½ cup water

TOPPING:

⅓ cup apple jelly (I used Jelly Queens)

1 jar marinated Australian goat and feta cheese

Directions

SWEET FIG CARAMELIZED ONION BACON JAM:

1. In medium saucepan, heat vegetable oil. Add diced onions and cook until they start to brown. Add garlic, black pepper, red pepper, and coriander. Cook for 2 minutes, then add figs. Stir to mix all ingredients together. Pour in vinegar, bringing to a boil. Add brown sugar. Lower heat and cook for additional 5 minutes until syrup forms.

2. Cook diced bacon until golden brown and crispy. Add to pot, stir.

3. Remove from heat and set aside for topping.

QUICK-PICKLED OKRA:

1. Prep okra by trimming the tops, washing, and cutting them in half.

2. Into a jar, smash cloves. Add pickling spice and both sprigs of herbs. Stand okra into the jar, set aside.

3. In a small pot, add white vinegar, sugar, cayenne, water, and salt. Bring to boil, then reduce heat and simmer for 3 minutes. Add liquid to the jar of fresh okra and seal tightly with a lid.

4. Cool at room temp for 30 minutes.

QUICK-PICKLED MUSTARD SEEDS:

1. In a saucepan, add apple cider vinegar, water, sugar, salt, and yellow mustard seeds.

2. Bring to boil, then reduce heat and simmer for 30 minutes.

3. Add thinly sliced shallots, remove from heat, cool and serve.

BACON:

1. Prep bacon and cut into desired slices or lardons. Rub with meat seasoning. Set aside and prepare the breading for deep frying the bacon.

"Food to me is like life...There are many levels to it, but it's all in how you choose to use them."

—Deborah Thomas

DIRECTIONS CONTINUED

2. Add flour in the first pan. Add beaten eggs and water in the second pan. Add chicken breading in the third pan.

3. Dredge each bacon slice in flour, shaking off excess. Then, dip in the egg mixture to cover. Lastly, dredge in the chicken breading.

4. Deep fry until golden and light floating. Remove and drain on paper towel.

ASSEMBLY:

1. To plate, place chicken-fried bacon on plate.

2. Top with jam, fresh micros, marinated goat cheese, quick pickled okra, and mustard seeds.

This is an angelic Bacon and Pork Belly Cinnamon Roll with a Bacon Halo. Japanese Pancakes are infused with a Bacon Peppermint Jam served over a Bacon Pork Belly Sausage Patty, featuring my 3 wise men: Peppermint Coffee Glaze, Creme de Menthe Mascarpone, and Strawberry Almond Coulis. Enjoy and Joyeux Noel!

Cook Time: 45 Minutes | Makes 8 servings

Head Cook:
Jack MacMurray

Team Name:
Jack Mac

Ingredients

BACON PEPPERMINT JAM:
1 pound smoked bacon, diced small

1 cup diced yellow onion

½ cup crushed peppermint candies

½ cup brown sugar

¼ cup coffee

2 tablespoons bourbon

2 tablespoons balsamic vinegar

Dash cinnamon & nutmeg

JAPANESE PANCAKES:
6 tablespoons cake flour

1 teaspoon baking powder

4 large egg whites

½ teaspoon cream of tartar

¼ cup sugar

1 teaspoon vanilla extract

Milk, as needed

BACON SAUSAGE PATTIES:
1 pound smoked bacon

½ pound pork belly, cooked

PORK BELLY CINNAMON ROLL:
12 ounces pork belly, cooked, cut into strips

1 cup maple syrup

1 teaspoon cinnamon

BACON HALO:
1 pound smoked bacon, as needed

PEPPERMINT COFFEE GLAZE:
½ cup peppermint candies

1 cup black coffee

CREME DE MENTHE MASCARPONE:
8 ounces mascarpone

½ cup powdered sugar

Creme de menthe, as needed

STRAWBERRY ALMOND COULIS:
1 pound strawberries, hulled

1 cup sugar

1 tablespoon almond extract

Zest and juice of 1 lemon

Directions

BACON PEPPERMINT JAM:
1. Render bacon until crispy, strain fat.
2. Add onions and cook till soft.
3. Add candies, brown sugar, coffee, bourbon, balsamic, cinnamon, and nutmeg. Reduce until thickened.
4. Purée.

JAPANESE PANCAKES:
1. Mix dry cake flour and baking powder.
2. Whisk in milk and vanilla to a thick pancake batter.
3. Whisk egg whites, cream of tartar, and sugar until stiff peaks.
4. Fold into batter in three stages.
5. Make pancakes as needed for build.

BACON SAUSAGE PATTIES:
1. Grind bacon and pork belly together.
2. Season and form patties.
3. Sear off for build.

PORK BELLY CINNAMON ROLL:
1. Take ¼" sliced pork belly and roll tightly together.
2. Stick with toothpicks to keep the circle together.
3. Mix maple syrup with nutmeg.
4. Bake for 15 minutes and glaze with maple syrup cinnamon mixture multiple times while finishing in the oven.
5. Set aside for build.

BACON HALO:
1. Lay out bacon slices and pound lightly, evenly.
2. Spray mason jar and wrap bacon slice around and stick with toothpicks to hold in place.
3. Bake until evenly crisp.
4. Set aside for build.

PEPPERMINT COFFEE GLAZE:
1. Place coffee and peppermints in a saucepot and reduce slightly.

CREME DE MENTHE MASCARPONE:
1. Whisk softened mascarpone, powdered sugar, and creme de menthe until smooth.

> *"You don't need a silver fork to eat good food."*
>
> —Paul Prudhomme

DIRECTIONS CONTINUED

STRAWBERRY ALMOND COULIS:

1. Place strawberries, sugar, lemon juice and zest, and almond extract into saucepot and reduce until thickened.

2. Strain and reserve.

ASSEMBLY:

1. Assemble on a plate with Bacon Sausage Patty first, then 1 pancake.

2. Top with Bacon Jam, then another pancake.

3. Place Pork Belly Cinnamon Roll to the side.

4. Place the Bacon Ring on top of the pancake stack.

5. Garnish with three sauces: Peppermint Coffee Glaze, Creme de Menthe Mascarpone, and Strawberry Almond Coulis.

Bacon Sweet Arancini with Bacon Bourbon Sauce Anglaise

Head Cook:
Jean-Paul Lavallee

Team Name:
Chef Jean-Paul The Bacon
Whisperer
Gulfport, MS

Cook Time: 45 Minutes | Makes 8 servings

Ingredients

RISOTTO:
2½ cups whole milk
2½ cups heavy cream
2 cups arborio rice
¼ cup orange juice
1 vanilla bean
1 pinch salt
¼ pound bacon, rendered
¼ cup dry fruits

½ cup turbinado sugar

BACON JAM:
1 pound bacon
1 cup of sugar
⅓ cup orange juice
¼ cup dry fruits

ARANCINI:
3 cups graham cracker crumbs
2 eggs

¼ cup milk
4 cups oil

**BACON BOURBON
ANGLAISE SAUCE:**
3 cups cream
3 ounces bourbon
Vanilla bean
½ cup sugar
6 egg yolks

Directions

RISOTTO:
1. In a pot, cook the arborio rice with the milk, heavy cream, sugar, orange juice, vanilla bean, and sautéed bacon.
2. Cook until tender and let cool.

BACON JAM:
1. Render bacon and add the sugar with the orange juice and dried fruits. Let cool.

ARANCINI:
1. Make quenelle stuffed with the Bacon Jam.
2. Dip in egg wash and graham cracker crumbs.
3. Fry at 350°F in oil and reserve.

**BACON BOURBON
SAUCE ANGLAISE:**
1. Bring the cream, bourbon, and vanilla bean to simmer.

2. Whisk the egg yolks and sugar until it is almost white.
3. Add the warm cream and milk to the egg mixture, then put back on fire until it thickens.

ASSEMBLY:
1. Dress with an array of fresh fruits and bacon and citrus fruits zest and serve.

"Cooking is like love. It should be entered into with abandon or not at all."

—Harriet Van Horne

Bradshaw, Aaron

My culinary training began in my grandmother's kitchen and continued on through a career in kitchens and restaurants for the last 27 years. I have experienced fast-paced, high volume restaurants, as well as smaller, more intimate catering opportunities. The one truth I've always found is that the food will always be my best interpreter in how much I truly love the industry, and the guests that I have the opportunity to serve out of our amazing little food truck, Crissy's Pub Style.

Bunter, Christoper

Christopher is a graduate of the Culinary Program at Portage College in Lac La Biche, Alberta. He began his career at 16 working in local hotels and pizzerias, moving on to larger hotel and camp setting kitchens. Finding a calling in the education sector where he contributed to the culinary workings of the University of Manitoba and University of Alberta, he has called Edmonton Public schools home since 2013, obtaining his Education Degree in 2020. His passion for burgers allowed him to broaden his skills at Woodshed Burgers in Edmonton during the summers.

Burton, Suzanne

I grew up in Alabama and my mom was a traditional southern cook who taught me how to cook from the time I was 10 years old. As I have gotten older, I have made healthier food choices. There are so many good things to eat that are good for you! Just because food is healthy doesn't mean it doesn't have flavor!

Calkins, David

Team Burger Republic from Nashville, TN, proudly serving our custom blend of certified angus beef burgers in Music City! Rated Top 10 Burger Restaurant in the USA by TripAdvisor.

Carberg, Daniel

A full-time college music professor and professional musician located in Keene New Hampshire, I have a long history of cooking meals for friends and family. My love of cooking landed me a guest spot on *The Drew Barrymore Show*'s "Cookbook Club" segment. In the past few years, I have placed in several national recipe contests. I love traveling, trying new cuisine, and meeting interesting people. In 2022 I was a finalist in the Bacon category at the World Food Championships.

Carlisle, Scott

I found my love for cooking over an open fire on a BBQ grill. I dabbled with local BBQ competitions for a few years and now I am a member of KCBS, a certified judge and compete in over a dozen events a season. I occasionally cater for friends and family at graduation and other parties. I come from a big family of great cooks, and they have inspired me the most.

Chatila, Sultan

I run a supper club called Tano's at 8, an underground dining experience based in Dubai focused on Mediterranean cuisine. I am a home-grown chef, cooking from my experiences and travels, and I base my cooking on nostalgic food from my childhood. Having competed in the Battle of the Burgers Dubai Edition, hosted by Cucina del Sul, and winning the event, I also enjoyed participating in the World Food Championships Burger Battle in Dallas and coming out in 3rd place globally.

Cheek, Morgan

We're Sweet Cheek's Pit BBQ, a husband-and-wife team from Muscle Shoals, AL. We started competing in Backyard BBQ in 2016 with only a couple of contests close to home. We really got fired up in 2017, cooking in as many competitions as possible. In the past few years, we've averaged 15–20 competitions a year. We began branching out into ancillaries to spice things up and have really enjoyed it! Burger is definitely our favorite.

Coe, Stephen

I'm a competitive chef whose 30 years of award-winning, Olympic-style competitions in culinary and pastries have led me to be an elite in my field. There are many chefs, but none with the drive and experience I have gained. I stand alone! I surround myself with only the best people and products, allowing me to have the cutting edge above the rest. I provide a rustic style of plating through modern and trendy techniques. Gatherings from intimate, multi-course tasting menus to multi-person customized events, we are up for the challenge! "Defined palate" is the mentality of the tight network of rogue chefs that I surround myself with and we are fearless industry professionals who stretch the limits, challenges, and boundaries...we're mavericks! I pride myself by providing excellence in service and execution. I support local purveyors and bring farm to table to reality! Limitless is the fuel that feeds me!

Cooper, Wayne

I'm a nine-time World Food Championship qualifier, 2018 Best Chef of Tangipahoa Parish, and love everything about food. Growing up in south Louisiana gave me the opportunities to learn my trade in an area famous for our cuisine. Surrounded by the some of the best cooks in the world (yes, I said world), I studied their techniques and stole many of their ideas. I was truly blessed to be raised here and I believe it's a true gift from God to have learned behind such talent.

D'Ambrosio, Thomas (Tommy)

Chef Thomas D'Ambrosio is a graduate from the Culinary Institute of America and has over a decade of fine dining experience. He was also crowned *Chopped* Champion on The Food Network in January of 2019 on the episode, "Tacos and Tequila." He completed his apprenticeship at the Greenbrier in West Virginia under certified Master Chef, Richard Rosendale. Chef Thomas has competed and took home the gold in many culinary competitions across the country, including Skills USA Nationals in Kansas City, where he placed first place in the nation, winner of the Scottsdale Culinary Fest Burger Battle for two years, Phoenix New Times Best Burger, Devoured Culinary Classic People's Choice, and more. Being born and raised in Arizona, Chef Thomas was happy to come back to his hometown and start, own, and operate Aioli Gourmet Burgers, Modern Tortilla, and Oak Wood Fire Pizza. Chef Thomas also graduated from NAU with a bachelor's degree in Hotel Restaurant Management in 2009.

Daniell, Neil

Neil and his wife, Erica, are the owners of KirbyG's® Diner in McDonough, Georgia. Besides winning the 2018 World Burger Championship, Neil and his team placed 4th in the world during the 2019 World Burger Competition and have won many awards for both burgers and bacon. You can also see him compete for $100,000 on CNBC's *Final Table New Orleans*, as well as his appearance on *Atlanta Eats* and the *Travel Channel: Best in Food* episode in 2018.

Desimeur, Thibaud

The most beautiful stories are those that are written between friends. This story begins with an encounter of four boys who share the same passion for cooking and the mad desire to leave their names in the history of the burger. After reaching the France objective, it was unthinkable not to aim for the world title. Mixing cultures, origins, and experiences, it was natural for us to come together to create a strong team to create our American dream. Thibaud, Benoit, Nicolas, and Joannes—a SO FRENCHY quartet—are built for victory.

Douglas, Ramon

I'm just a California native that loves eating burgers and creating burgers. Born and raised in Altadena, CA, after high school, I didn't know what I wanted to do. I was in and out of different colleges for years until a friend of mine suggested I go to culinary school. I never looked back… Disney World, country clubs, working as a private chef, and competing in burger contests were in my future.

Duplantis, Susanne

Louisiana native Susanne Duplantis is an award-winning chef, restaurant veteran, creator of the food waste blog, *Makeover My Leftover*, and author of "Lagniappe Leftovers." She has competed in national and international cooking competitions. Susanne works as a recipe developer for national brands, conducts food waste workshops and cooking demos, has appeared on Netflix, Food Network, Tamron Hall, Rachael Ray and hosted a monthly cooking segment on a CBS affiliate TV station for five years.

Dye, Jon

I have been teaching Culinary Arts at Waynesville Career Center for the past 20 years. I'm originally from Waynesville and have loved returning here after traveling and working in the hospitality industry when I was younger. I enjoy my students' success and how they use the things we teach them as they move on to chef school after my program or successful careers.

Elliott, Dave

Dave Elliott is a competition chef from Olathe, KS. Originally from Minnesota, he later moved to Kansas City where he found his love of BBQ and outdoor cooking. Although he specializes in outdoor cooking, he has competed in the Dessert, Pasta, Burger, and Steak categories at the World Food Championships. In 2013, he won the whole thing and became the World Food Champion. In 2022, he won the World Burger Champion. He has also won several BBQ contests and has received over 150 awards. He has appeared on national television and on local stations across the country.

Elliot, Karen

I'm a member of a cooking team called Pirates of the Grillibbean from Bartlett, TN. Our team has been together for almost six years, and it's made up of family members and friends. I've enjoyed cooking for most of my life and I find it exciting to cook for a competitive team. I enjoy planning out our competition entries to ensure we have a high-quality product. Our team competes in cooking competitions locally for charities, such as Memphis Paws and Ronald McDonald House.

Emery, Mark

As Senior Manager of Product Development, I have been given the opportunity to use my passion for food and create great private brand deli items for Walmart customers. I was chosen to captain Walmart's Private Brand Culinary Team of Jackie Nartowicz (Bakery), Peter Kuhr (Produce), and Stephen O'Brien (Grocery) in the 2019 World Food Championships. Education in the culinary arts from Grand Rapids Community College and a food marketing degree from Western Michigan University led me to professional roles as executive/corporate chef, product development, and sales management of retail, food service, and commercial equipment businesses. I grew up living aboard a sailboat cruising the Bahamas prior to attending high school and college in West Michigan and now I live in Northwest Arkansas with my wife Katie and our three children Max, Naomi, and Zeke.

Evans, Rebecka

At Home with Rebecka has been my blog home since 2010. I'm a wife, mother, grandmother, and an award-winning competitive cook. My site offers hundreds of heirloom and contest recipes made with the freshest ingredients for the whole family. I'm living my best life; a culinary journey of comfort and style in Denver, Colorado with my sweet husband Blake. We are blessed with five grown children and eight beautiful grandchildren. The joy of food blogging, recipe creation, food sport, and learning the art of food photography and styling has been a labor of love. I won my first TV competition appearance on the Food Network's *Clash of the Grandmas* "Home Sweet Grandma" episode, taking home a cash prize of $10 thousand dollars and I haven't stopped winning since! My talent goes beyond the kitchen and onto the stage as a trained classical vocalist. I've performed in many professional productions, and my second passion aside from cooking is singing opera.

Fortin, Wade

After a three-year hiatus away from the world of Food Sport, Wade Fortin and Andrew Wiegand rejoined the fray of the World Food Championships once again to attempt to claim their 3rd world title in the Burger category. Lately, Wade has been busy on the sponsor side taking the reins of the marketing department for Bull Outdoor Products Inc.

Giovannoni, Jonathan

Five-time Canadian Bacon Champion, *Chopped Canada* Junior Winner, and four-time Top 10 Finalist at WFC Bacon Category. I'm also a motivational speaker, philanthropist, and owner of One Oak Kitchen LLC in Miami, FL.

Hess, Andrew

Andrew is a graduate of the Culinary Program at The Northern Alberta Institute of Technology (NAIT) in 2005. He has found opportunities in resorts, wineries, and restaurants in Alberta and British Columbia. In 2014, he earned a Bachelor of Education degree and has been working as a chef instructor for Edmonton public schools, providing knowledge and skills to hundreds of students every year.

Hindman, Stephen

I'm the owner, designer, builder, and executive chef of Stacked, A Montana Grill in downtown Billings, MT. My passion for food and people of all cultures led to building a cooking style that combines the best of Montana (Western) foods with the endless flavors the world has to offer. I simply love taking dishes people know and reintroducing them with innovative layers of flavors. There simply isn't anything more satisfying than the glow on someone's face when you excite their palate with something wonderful.

Hodgins, Dan

I have been competing in Professional Food Sport since 2009 and won multiple awards. The passion and drive to cook has always been in my heart.

Hogan, Michael

My recipe is from my 6th appearance at the World Food Championships. I am the chief cook for the Team Spice Your Life Rub Your Meats and owner of the catering company of the same name. Through the catering company, I also offer cooking classes and private dinner parties. I'm a former Traeger Influencer of two-and-a-half years, a former KCBS Certified Barbeque Judge, and a former Board Member of The Greater Omaha Barbeque Society. Currently a certified EAT Judge, I also have several cooking awards, from BBQ to bacon. I've competed in the Omaha Beer and Bacon Festival four times winning twice. Won two different Culinary Fight Club's Tasters Choice. I have qualified for World Food Championships seven times, and in 2022 was ranked 6th in the World of Bacon.

Holter, Damon

Damon Holter is the owner of Croix Valley Foods, an award-winning manufacturer of BBQ sauces and seasonings found in over 3,000 locations across the globe. Using his flavors in the competitive arena of food sport, Damon has garnered hundreds of awards, including multiple World Championship titles.

Jackman, Drew

Team Burger Republic from Nashville, TN, proudly serving our custom blend of certified angus beef burgers in Music City! Rated Top 10 Burger Restaurant in the USA by TripAdvisor.

James, Jordan

My baking journey began when my mother proposed a *Cupcake Wars*-style challenge over a spring break to fill the time away from school. I loved the show and threw myself into the challenge, baking more than 200 cupcakes over the week. Without any planning as to what to do with the cakes, we passed them around to grateful neighbors and friends, one of whom suggested I sell them as a means of paying for a summer fashion camp in New York. That was the spark. Five years later, Cupcakes by Jordan James has grown to a business that serves the cupcake needs of weddings, farmers markets, and special events throughout the Midwest. When I'm not baking, you can find me performing on stage, playing the mellophone and French horn in my high school's marching and concert bands, sewing, spending time with my friends, or preparing for a future in fashion design.

Jett, Staci

I'm a born-and-raised country cook. I was taught how to cook and bake from scratch at the heels of my Grandmother. I love to experiment and believe the kitchen is the heart of the family. I'm also a butcher, hunter, and fisherman. I can take any animal from field to table and I have processed deer for local hunters in my home meat room for around 10 years. I'm known on the competition BBQ circuit and am a brand ambassador for KYSEK Ice Chests. My personality is like my cooking: bright, fun loving, and spicy. I have competed and won Travel Channel's *American Grilled: Louisville* and have appeared on Food Network's *Chopped: Grill Masters*.

Joeckel, Tamie

A four-time qualifier for World Food Championships in Bacon, Tamie Joeckel has a passion for cooking! A glam-ma "Mimi" to Abigail, Madeline, and Lowen James, she hails from a 5th generation, cattle raising Texas family and is a boot scootin', self-taught home cook. Friends and family know that food will always be the center of any event she hosts. Her cooking style is an amalgamation of Southern comfort, Tex-Mex, Cajun, and other flavors she's experienced in her global travels. One of her favorite things to do is cook heirloom recipes with her grandgirls, passing on the traditions!

Katz, Lauren

Lauren Katz is the Executive Chef at The Difference Baker in Ashburn, and the winner of ABC's first season of *The Great American Baking Show*. Lauren has competed in over 50 culinary competitions, including The Pillsbury Bake Off, Sutter Home's Build a Better Burger, The Gilroy Garlic Festival, and the World Food Championships. She has appeared on *The Kitchen*, *Good Morning America*, *Great Day Washington*, and *Pickler and Ben*. Her recipes have been featured in several magazines. Lauren has a BFA in Painting and Printmaking from Virginia Commonwealth University.

Keiles, Doug

I am an eight-time WFC competitor, finishing 2nd place in 2013 and 2017 in Burger, and 8th in 2018. I got back to the Top 10 in 2021 in Sandwich with a 4th place finish. I have been cooking BBQ for 20 years and I have won Grand Championships in BBQ, kosher BBQ, Grilling, Bacon, Burgers, and Dessert. In 2019, I was Grilling Team of the Year in the Northeast BBQ Society. I currently run a shared commercial kitchen and a Saturday-only BBQ stand in Gloucester, MA.

Kennedy, Linwood

I was born and raised in Atlanta, Georgia, where I had the pleasure of being owner of an Atlanta-based catering company, Eliza Catering, since 2002. After completing culinary school at Le Cordon Bleu, in 2014, I moved up the ladder as Sous Chef for Executive Chef Jernard Wells (two-time winner on *Cutthroat Kitchen*). In November 2014, I competed in the 2014 World Food Championship Pasta Challenge, placing in the top 10. In 2017, I had the pleasure working with celebrity chef Elliott Farmer (winner of *Cutthroat Kitchen* Season 8). In 2019, I became the Chapter President of the National Black Chef Association (NBCA). In May 2019, I competed in the Blended Burger Challenge, where I won People's Choice Award. I went on to compete in the 2019 World Food Championships, placing in the top 10 at sixth place in the bacon category.

Lavallee, Jean-Paul

Originally from Quebec City Canada, I began my career during the summer of 1984. While working as a cook at La Grande Table de Serge Bruyere in Quebec City in 1987, I served President Ronald Reagan and President Mikhail Gorbachev; it was quite an experience! In January 2000, I moved to Cleveland, Ohio to be the chef de cuisine at the famous City Club of Cleveland. Two years later, I moved south to Mississippi and it's been my home ever since.

MacMurray, Jack

Madaris, Derrick

I have been cooking with my mother since I was eight years old. We're French, so we love cooking savory dishes and using lots of butter. I competed in my first professional food competition at the age of 21. I currently work at Table 65 Bistro as a chef in New Richmond, Wisconsin, and I'm also a full-time nursing student.

Malla, Jayson

I was born and raised on the beautiful island of Oahu, HI. After graduating at Le Cordon Bleu Culinary in Portland, Oregon, my culinary career started at the esteemed Kahala Resort in Honolulu before expanding my horizons and skills, all the way to the famed Greenbrier Resort in White Sulphur Springs, West Virginia and the Rosewood Hotel and Spa in Menlo Park, California. I returned to Oahu in 2010 and worked at the Trump International Hotel Waikiki and most recently at Aulani Disney Resort and Spa before becoming the Chef de Cuisine at Sheraton Kona's signature restaurant, Rays on the Bay. Currently, I work for Bon Appetit Management Company as Chef De Cuisine for Food at Google in Mountain View, CA. I like to reinvent the classics into delectable, new culinary creations and capture that memorable experience that you've had with familiar flavors.

Martinez, Joseph

Born and raised in Brownsville, Texas, Chef Joseph Martinez brings his native Texan roots to the forefront of his culinary point of view. Joseph was classically trained in French technique and cuisine at Le Cordon Bleu before beginning his career at the Walt Disney World Resort in Orlando, Florida.

Following his experience at Disney, Chef Joseph returned to Texas to join the Silo Restaurant Group in San Antonio. Over the course of an eight-year tenure at Silo, Chef Joseph contributed to the successful opening of three restaurants and oversaw operations at Silo Prime & Terrace Oyster Bar. At Silo, Joseph developed an appreciation for handmade pastas that he incorporated throughout his menus and daily specials.

In 2021, Chef Joseph joined the Marriott Rivercenter and Riverwalk hotels as the Sous Chef of Tributary, the hotel's signature restaurant. Joseph's technique-driven cuisine was immediately infused into the Tributary menu which takes inspiration from the regions and local products of Texas. During his time as Sous Chef, Joseph gained local and nationwide notoriety as the back-to-back winner of the San Antonio Burger Showdown. Joseph's local win earned him the chance to compete at the World Food

Championships in Dallas, Texas in 2022. Joseph's award winning "Elote Burger" finished in 8th place overall during the competition which featured competitors from around the globe.

Chef Joseph now moves into the role of Senior Sous Chef of the Marriott Rivercenter and Riverwalk hotels. In this role, Joseph leads the culinary operations five restaurants and cafes, including Tributary. Beyond his role with Marriott, Chef Joseph is heavily involved in the local food community where he sits on the board of Chef's Cooperative, a local nonprofit dedicated to raising money for local farms and small businesses by participating in community events.

Moody, Travis

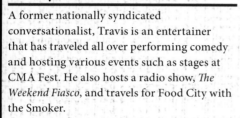

A former nationally syndicated conversationalist, Travis is an entertainer that has traveled all over performing comedy and hosting various events such as stages at CMA Fest. He also hosts a radio show, *The Weekend Fiasco*, and travels for Food City with the Smoker.

Travis started experimenting with foods as a wee lad, which as he began to grow, he started cooking for himself and others...Thankfully no one was injured or died from his dishes. His mom says he'll make a good housewife one day. Travis has traveled to several countries where he's learned various dishes, from pasta making in Italy, macarons in France, Koshary in Egypt, creole in Louisiana, etc. He craves to try different foods and experience different cultures. Travis is normally known for his BBQ abilities. Travis likes educating people on cooking, showing them new options and ways of preparing food.

Muterspaugh, Rick

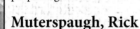

I started competing on the Kansas City Barbeque Society circuit with Smokedout BBQ in 2015. In 2018, I was introduced to the World Food Championships and competed for two years with Smokedout BBQ and Josh and Jessica Dae. In 2021, I competed for the first time as a head cook in the Steak category. I finished in 4th place. In 2022, I entered the Burger category, made the finals, and finished 11th overall. I also compete in the Steak Cookoff Association and have been to the World Championships in Fort Worth two times.

Norem, Jennifer

I've been cooking since I was 16. I've always had a love for cooking and my passion has always been cooking delicious dishes and bringing smiles to the faces of my family and friends. I love creating and cooking a variety of dishes, from old school, street food and comfort food to my heritage of Polish and Italian. I love the pressure and the adrenal rush competition cooking brings me. You're not only cooking with the best of the best, but you're pushing yourself beyond your comfort zone to give the best that you got. When you're cooking against professional chefs, private chefs, international chefs, and other home cooks, you're cooking and showcasing your talent to prove you're the best of the best within time limits. The food sport family is just that, a great group of people who come together and show great sportsmanship, love, and friendship and we all consider each other family. I have met and built a lot of great friendships I otherwise wouldn't have if it wasn't for the food sport competition. The most important thing about competition is it lets me showcase my love and passion for cooking.

Ogiya, Atsuko

I started my career as a Head Chef of Shogun Burger in April 2016, opening my first branch in Shinjuku. After the successful launch, I opened several branches in Tokyo, Kanazawa, Miyako Island, Chiba, and Yokohama, and I have been overseeing all those stores as an Executive Chef. I'm also responsible for coming up with all new and seasonal menus, and my creations have been often featured in Japanese TV. SHOGUN BURGER was originally started as a Yakiniku (Korean styled BBQ) house "Dai Shogun," then expanded as one of most successful artisanal burger chains by utilizing skills and knowledge of meat. Now my team and I are looking at even more different brands such as café, diner, and so on to possibly open in near future.

Otto, Ron

I'm the head cook for Daddy O's Surf City BBQ. We have been competing in BBQ competitions for over 20 years and have won many awards for our BBQ and sauces. We won the 2016 San Diego Bull Burger Battle Champion. We're also a five-time World Food Championships Competitor and three-time finalist. I own an arsenal of smokers and have traveled the US tasting the best BBQ in the world. I collect vintage BBQ books and I am a vintage motorcycle enthusiast.

Perrotta, Jose

Passionate for food since a young kid, I started cooking in my mom's little Italian restaurant in Santo Domingo, Dominican Republic. It was there where my passion and dedication towards gastronomy started to grow. I went on to create three of the most popular burger restaurants in DR. I focus on creating exceptional experiences for my customers and mind-blowing combinations.

Przybylski, George

George Przybylski is the Pit Master of the Bang Bang BBQ Competition Food Sport Team. He has been competing in Food Sport for 12 years. He began his journey with a few friends from work, which then evolved into George separating from the original team to begin a new journey with his wife, son, and cousin. Bang Bang BBQ was born! When he's not competing on the foodie circuit, he works with his local Scouts BSA Troop by volunteering as a Cooking Merit Badge Counselor and showing his scouts that camp food doesn't have to be boring. He loves cooking for friends and family to hone his skills and prepare for his next contest.

Quintana, Hiram

Restaurateur, executive chef, owner, and operator of Stave and Stable, Sizzle, and The Forge Coffeehouse Corporate, and executive chef of J.J. Ratigan Brewing Company.

Radjou, Peter

Chef Radjou comes from the southern part of India and has traveled widely to many parts of the world. He enjoys cooking, eating, and entertaining others with his multi-cuisine expertise. His style of cooking is inspired by many cultures. He loves fusion cooking, which influences his creativity when creating new dishes.

Saunders, Anna (Davis)

Chef Anna is a self-made professional chef, world traveler, food enthusiast and entrepreneur. My culinary competition streak started after auditioning for *Chopped at Home* (an offshoot from *Chopped*), making it to the finals in NYC, and then leaving with the grand prize. From there, I competed in several online recipe contests and local and state competitions, bringing home more blue ribbons. Competing at WFC in 2019 was definitely a highlight, and I couldn't have been more excited to place in the Top 5 in the Bacon category. Cooking is my passion and receiving the Chef of the Year award in my city in 2021 really sealed my love for giving this gift to others.

Sheppard, Sandi

I began competing in both online contests and cook off competitions in 2010 after a long career as the Advertising, Marketing and PR Director for Oklahoma's first Pari-Mutuel Race Track, then switching to become the Art Director for a sign company, designing everything from yard signs to billboards and vehicle wraps. After my first national cook off competition in 2010, I discovered that I was very competitive in the kitchen arena; I loved the competitors and the rush of excitement competing, and have never looked back!

My World Food Championships (WFC) journey began in 2013 winning the WFC qualifier "OKC Bull Burger Battle" for both pros and home cooks, and a Bull Outdoor sponsorship to the World Food Championship in Vegas and bragging rights as the 1st female home cook to win a Bull Burger Battle competition! I've been honored to place in the World Food Championships Top 10 categories four times, for World Recipe in 2014 and placed 2nd-In-The-World in WFC Burger category in 2015. I won the WFC Taste of America Oklahoma state division in 2018, finishing 8th-In-The-World in Chili, and 2nd again in WFC Burger 2021.

I've won many other cooking competitions over the years, including the National Maple Leaf Farms "Strut Your Duck" contest in both 2013 and 2015, and being winner, placing and/or a finalist in many other contests since 2010.

Shive, Tommy

2017 WFC World Burger Champion, 2021 WFC Top 10 Burger (5th), 2022 WFC Top 10 Burger (10th).

Taffel, Jodi

As a working actor in Hollywood for 30 years, I've realized that being artistic doesn't mean being contained to just one art form. I found that I could unleash even more artistic creativity in the kitchen. And I don't need anyone's permission to do it (i.e., no audition process)! And competition cooking seemed to be a natural progression.

After five times in the Top 10, I finally won the title of Bacon World Champion in 2019. And since the 2020 WFC was canceled due to the pandemic, one could argue that I held that title longer than anyone else! At Final Table, I won the 2nd round and ended up placing 2nd overall by half a point. That half a point is what brought me back.

Thomas, Deborah

I was born in Gulfport, MS as the fourth child of 13 siblings. Being creative wasn't much a challenge for me, and having to learn how to cook was part of the plan growing up. I eventually stepped into the casino culinary field, where I got lots of hands-on training from some of the best local chefs. From buffet style to fine dining, my passion to cook and still stay true to my southern swag has been an experience. I have competed and placed and serval cooking competitions, and I even tried a little ice carving. During my culinary journey, I worked at one of the best casinos on the Gulf Coast, Island View Casino & Resort, where I've been for 16 years. Entering into WFC, I assisted as Sous Chef in 2016. I gained my own Golden Ticket in Taste of America 2019, winning first place for State of Mississippi. Changing the game, I then entered the Bacon Category in 2021 and 2022, finally making it to the Top Ten! I started saying, "Everything got to be better with bacon."

Todora, Paula

From Savannah to Scotland, I've made my mark in the competitive cooking world among the best home cooks and professional chefs around. Holding the title of Brand Ambassador for numerous major food brands has provided me with priceless experiences, friendships, and opportunities. Cooking is not my job, but my PASSION!

Trupiano, Tore

Woolf, Andrea

Just a butcher by trade and an inspired amateur chef who is now hooked on competing in food competitions.

INDEX

Note: Page numbers in bold indicate all-star chef bios. Page numbers in *bold italics* indicate interviews.